A DAY IN THE DEATH OF JOE EGG

A Play

by

PETER NICHOLS

LONDON
NEW YORK SYDNEY TORONTO HOLLYWOOD

SAMUEL FRENCH LTD, 26 SOUTHAMPTON STREET, STRAND, LONDON, W.C.2, or their authorized agents, issue licences to amateurs to give performances of this play on payment of a fee. **The fee must be paid, and the licence obtained, before a performance is given.**

Licences are issued subject to the understanding that it shall be made clear in all advertising matter that the audience will witness an amateur performance; and that the names of the authors of plays shall be included in all announcements and on all programmes.

The royalty fee indicated below is subject to contract and subject to variation at the sole discretion of Samuel French Ltd.

The publication of this play must not be taken to imply that it is necessarily available for performance by amateurs or professionals, either in the British Isles or overseas. Amateurs intending production must, in their own interests, make application to Samuel French Ltd or their authorized agents, for consent before starting rehearsals or booking a theatre or hall.

Fee for one performance by amateurs in the British Isles	£7
Fee for a second consecutive performance at the same theatre or hall	£6
Fee for each subsequent consecutive performance at the same theatre or hall	£5

In territories overseas the fee quoted above may not apply. A quotation will be given upon application to the authorized agents, or direct to SAMUEL FRENCH LTD.

Applications to perform the play by professionals should be made to Margaret Ramsay Ltd, 14 Goodwin's Court, London, W.C.2.

GB 573 01084 6

MADE AND PRINTED IN GREAT BRITAIN BY
LATIMER TREND AND CO. LTD, WHITSTABLE
MADE IN ENGLAND

A DAY IN THE DEATH OF JOE EGG

First produced at the Citizens Theatre, Glasgow, on the 9th May 1967. Subsequently produced at the Comedy Theatre, London on the 20th July 1967, with the following cast of characters.

(in order of their appearance)

BRI, Joe Melia
SHEILA, Zena Walker
JOE, Elaine Mileham *or* Susan Porter
PAM, Phyllida Law
FREDDIE, John Carson
GRACE, Joan Hickson

The Play directed by MICHAEL BLAKEMORE

Setting by Robin Pidcock

SYNOPSIS OF SCENES

The action takes place in the living-room of Bri's and Sheila's home

ACT I

An evening in winter

ACT II

Later the same night

Time—the present

ACT I

BRI AND SHEILA

SCENE—*The living-room in Bri's and Sheila's home.*

The room is pleasant and comfortable, furnished with a gallant collection of junk-shop bargains and H.P. modern. On the walls, which are plain, two paintings of cowboys are conspicuous. A door up C *leads to the hall and stairs, which can be seen when it is open. Another door up* R *leads to the kitchen. There is a window* R. *A bird in a cage is up* R, *a tank containing fish up* L, *and around the room are plants in pots.*

When the CURTAIN *rises, only the forestage is lit by a spot, and the room is invisible.* BRI *comes on from the wings down* L *without warning, moves* C *and shouts at the audience. He is thirty-three but looks younger, and is hardly ever at rest. He acts being maladroit, but the act is skilful. Clowning may give way to ineffectual hectoring and then self-piteous gloom.*

BRI. That's enough! (*He pauses, then almost at once shouts louder*) I said enough! (*He pauses, staring at the audience*) Another word and you'll all be here till five o'clock. Nothing to me, is it? I've got all the time in the world. (*He moves across* R *without taking his eyes off the audience*) I didn't even get to the end of the corridor before there was such a din all the other teachers started opening their doors as much as to say what the hell's going on there's SOMEBODY TALKING NOW! (*He pauses, staring again, like someone facing a mad dog*) Who was it? You? You, Mister Man? . . . I did not *accuse* you, I *asked* you. Someone in the back row? (*He stares dumbly for some seconds, relaxes, moves a few steps, shrugs*) You're the losers, not me. Who's that? (*He turns on them again*) Right—hands on heads! Come on, that includes you, put the comb away. Eyes front and sit up. All of you, sit up! (*He puts his own hands on his head for a while, watching for a move, waiting for a sound, then takes them down and suddenly roars*) Hands on head and eyes front! YOU I'm talking to! You'll be *tired* by the time I've finished. Stand on your seat. And keep your hands on your heads. Never mind what's going on outside, that joker at the back. Keep looking out here. Eyes front, hands on heads. (*He moves across to* L)

(*A bell rings*)

Who said MOVE? Nobody said move. Hands on heads. Next one to groan stands on the seat. We're going to have one minute's perfect silence before you go. (*He looks at his watch*) If we have to wait till midnight. (*He stands watching for some seconds*) That's nice. I like that. Now try to hold it just like that till I get to this machine-gun over here. (*He moves upstage, turning his back, then turns round again at once*) My fault, all right. Little joke. No more laughing. The noise from this class can be heard all over Bristol. (*He waits for silence, then looks at his watch, moving across. Suddenly he looks up, very angry again*) Who was that? Whoever did—that—can open the window before we all get gassed. Wait a minute! Three of you? what are you—a group? One go—one nearest the window. All the others, eyes front hands on heads. Right. (*He looks at his watch*) That characteristic performance from our friend near the window means we return to Gc. (*He looks up sharply*) Shall I make it *two* minutes? (*He looks down again. Ten seconds pass*) We could have had this sooner. Then we shouldn't be wasting time sitting here when we might be—well—let's all—think—what we might be doing—stead of sitting here when the rest have gone home—we could be . . . (*He is speaking quietly now, absently staring into space. A few more seconds pass. When he speaks again it is as if in a reverie*) Yes—eyes front—hands on breasts—STOP the laughter! WHO wants to start another minute? (*He looks at his watch, then up again*) And whatever the great joke it is that has so tickled your Stone Age sense of humour—when all my efforts have failed—save it till you're outside. I'm going to get my coat from the staff-room now. And you will be as quiet as mice—no, fish—till I get back. All right? I don't want to hear a sound. Not a bubble.

(BRI *moves* L, *pauses, then exits down* L. *The* LIGHTS *come up on the room.* SHEILA, *wearing trousers and pullover, enters from the kitchen with tea on a trolley. She is thirty-five, generously built, serious and industrious. When dressed for society, she can be captivating. She wheels the trolley* RC *and runs back to the kitchen door, pushing with her foot, keeping out an animal*)

SHEILA. Back, back, no, no. (*She shuts the door and returns* RC)

(*A door slams off up* L. SHEILA *starts pouring tea*)

(*Shouting*) Bri?

BRI (*off*) No.

SHEILA (*shouting*) Just got tea.

(BRI *enters up* C, *and moves to Sheila.* SHEILA *offers him a kiss. He takes it, then stands close, looking at her.* SHEILA *goes back to pouring tea and offers him his cup. He doesn't take it, so she looks at his face, then screams, nearly spilling the tea*)

What's that?

BRI. What?

SHEILA. On your face!

BRI. Where?

SHEILA. Near your eye.

BRI. What is it?

SHEILA. A black thing.

BRI. For Christ's sake . . .

SHEILA. A spider . . .
BRI. Shall I touch it?
SHEILA. A great black—get it off!
BRI. How?
SHEILA. Knock it off!

(BRI *takes it off, smiling*)

Ugh!
BRI (*putting it on the back of his hand and showing it to her*) I confiscated it.

(SHEILA *knocks it away angrily*)

From Terry Hodges.
SHEILA. Vicious pig!
BRI. He *is*. For thirteen.
SHEILA (*giving Bri his tea*) You, I mean.
BRI. In Religious Instruction.
SHEILA. It's not funny. (*She turns away from him*)
BRI. What I told *him*. (*Seeing he has done wrong*) Sweetheart . . . (*He approaches her from behind and kisses her neck*)
SHEILA. Get away!
BRI. Oh look . . .
SHEILA. Why d'you do it, Brian, honestly? You know that would upset me and the first thing you do . . .
BRI. Sorry, love.
SHEILA. I even kissed you.
BRI. Sorry. (*He drinks his tea*)

(SHEILA *also drinks her tea.* BRI *puts his cup down and kisses her again, then caresses her*)

Oh, love, if you knew how I'd been thinking of you . . .
SHEILA. You'll spill this tea.
BRI. Let's go to bed, come on.
SHEILA. Ow! Don't . . .
BRI. What?
SHEILA. Your hands are cold, you've only just come in . . .
BRI. Let's go to bed.
SHEILA. At quarter to five?
BRI. I came home early specially.
SHEILA. The usual time.
BRI. Yeah, but I was *going* to keep them in.
SHEILA. Who?
BRI. Four D.
SHEILA. Did you *say* you would?
BRI (*sitting* L *on the sofa*) Yes.
SHEILA (*sitting* L *on the sofa*) Then why didn't you?
BRI. I kept imagining our bed, our room, clothes strewn all over the place.

Sheila. When *are* you going to learn?

Bri. Waves breaking on a rocky shore.

Sheila. You must carry out your threats.

Bri. Fireworks in the sky.

Sheila. They'll never listen to you if you don't . . .

Bri. Champagne bottles going pop! Sugar. (*He rises, helps himself to sugar, then moves back to sofa*)

Sheila. You want bromide.

Bri. I want you. It's you I want. (*He turns, making a joke of it, pointing to her like the advertisement*) I want you. Kitchener, look. I want you.

(Sheila *smiles*. Bri *sits and drinks*)

Sheila. You should have kept them in.

Bri. I did for a bit. Then I went off to the staff room to fetch my coat, and suddenly couldn't face them any more, so I never went back. Wonder how long they sat there.

Sheila. Brian . . .

Bri. Terry Hodges, Fatty Brent—Glazebrook, the shop-steward—he's got a new watch. And of course Scanlon—(*shaking his head at the idea*)—the Missing Link. Pithecanthropus Erectus.

Sheila. Has he tried it lately?

Bri. Not with the teachers anyway.

Sheila. Only that once.

Bri. That was the only time it was reported.

Sheila. Poor girl.

Bri. Some of the older women might keep quiet. Hope for more.

Sheila. What happened to that girl?

Bri. Never heard of since.

Sheila. Not surprising.

Bri. Shortest teaching career on record. Thirty-five minutes.

(*They drink*)

No, I don't hate Scanlon any more. That's all a thing of the past. I just stare at him and wonder—is he only a monster of my own imagining? (*He puts on his Mad Doctor voice, not for the last time*) "Certainly, Nurse, he strangled a little girl, but that only means he's lonely. We must make him a mate."

(Sheila *smiles*. Bri *drinks again*)

No, you take this morning. I was on playground duty sipping my Nescafe, dreaming of a sudden painless road accident that would put an end to it all. Suddenly aware of the silence—too quiet for comfort. Few of the wilder elements sniggering and casting crafty glances. Whipped round in time to spot Scanlon sidling into the girls' bog. Went to the door and shouted: "That boy, out of it!" Saw this figure zipping up his flies in a panic. Not Scanlon at all.

Sheila. No!

BRI. No. This new supply teacher.
SHEILA. Oh, no.
BRI. Yes.
SHEILA. Funny that way?
BRI. Not a bit. He didn't know it was the girls'. Only *looks* about thirteen even from the front. (*He rises, takes a biscuit from the trolley and moves above the sofa*) Dresses like them too. Why can't he wear the right bloody uniform—tweedy jacket and leather elbows—so we'd know whose side he's on? (*He pauses and eats his biscuit*)
SHEILA. Never mind. You break up in two days.
BRI. I broke up years ago. (*He puts his hand on her shoulder*)

(SHEILA *removes his hand*)

Shall I put my gloves on?
SHEILA. What's the point of starting *now*? Joe's home any minute.
BRI (*moving* C) Well?
SHEILA. Well! She's got to be fed, bathed, exercised, put to bed. You know that.
BRI (*after a pause*) She can wait.
SHEILA. What?
BRI. Well, can't she?
SHEILA. Why should she?

(*There is a pause.* BRI *moves to the chaise* LC *and sits*)

Anyway, my rehearsal's at seven and I promised to paint some scenery before that. I shouldn't be late, but your dinner's in the oven. On automatic. Take it out any time after seven. You'd never believe the job I had finding a miniature bottle of Kirsch. In the local off-licence they offered Spanish Van Rose instead. Luckily I was going into town so I got it there. I had to take those old clothes into the Unmarried Mothers. They were only collecting moths.

(BRI *feels in his pockets*)

What are you looking for?
BRI. Matches.

(SHEILA *throws him a box from the coffee-table*)

(*Lighting a cigarette from his case*) Collecting moths? The Unmarried Mothers?
SHEILA. The clothes. The livestock's all been fed—the cats, the guinea-pigs, the goldfish, the stick-insects . . .

(*There is a pause*)

BRI. The ginger-beer plant?
SHEILA. All the plants. Oh, remember not to let the cats in. I found a flea in here again today. And this afternoon I did my Oxfam collection and looked after Jenny's children while she went to the Family Planning Clinic. Quite a day one way or another. What are you thinking?

Bri. Wondering if we could send our guinea-pig to the Family Planning Clinic. Or guinea-sow, should it be? (*He scratches himself, then jumps up*) I've got one now. (*He looks closely at the chaise for fleas*)

Sheila. If you've had a bad day, why don't you come with me?

Bri. Bad day? You ought to see the staff-room! Christmas Spirit nearly at breaking-point. Excuse me, I was under the impression that was my soap you're using—shove off—I beg your pardon?—shove off, matey—come outside and say that—grow up—no, I insist—come on . . . I sang: "Great tidings of comfort and joy." But it fell on stony ground. (*He moves to the sofa, sits, and takes her hand*) I said to my class: "Right—Christmas decorations—paper-chains." Deep voice from the back said: "Kids' stuff". I frowned at him and realized I'd never seen him before. Turned out he was the elder brother of one of the more backward boys. On the dole, he'd come in out of the cold, been sitting in classes all day, nobody'd noticed.

Sheila. Did you throw him out?

Bri. What for? (*Smiling at the recollection*) When he brought me up his paper-chain, he said: "You're not much good at teaching, are you, mate?"

Sheila. Oh, I should have hit him.

Bri. He meant it nicely. (*He smokes*) I must find something else.

Sheila (*rising and moving above the sofa*) Come with me to rehearsal. Do you good to get out, see some people.

Bri. What people? Freddie?

Sheila. Plenty of whisky afterwards.

Bri. I should want the whisky first—

Sheila. All right, first.

Bri. —if I had to talk to Freddie.

Sheila. All right.

Bri. If I had to watch you caper about with muck on your face.

Sheila. Shall I ring your mother and see if she's free?

Bri. Bloody hell! What a swinging prospect! My mother, Freddie . . .

Sheila. I seem to remember . . .

Bri. And all that kirsch bubbling away down there.

Sheila. I seem to remember it was you who introduced me to Freddie in the first place.

(*The door-bell rings*)

Bri. There's Joe. (*He rises and moves to the door up* c)

Sheila (*moving to the trolley*) Remember that. (*Shouting after Bri*) And at least I don't just sit about coining epigrams—wallowing in self-pity! At least I *do* something about it!

Bri. You and Freddie together, yea . . .

(Bri *exits, leaving the door partly open*)

Sheila (*shouting*) At least I try to make life work instead of . . . (*She breaks off and sighs, deeply, almost as though doing an exercise in relaxation*) Honestly. (*She puts the cups on the trolley, picks up a saucer, puts some milk in it, and moves to the door up* R. *To an invisible cat outside*) Get away from the door then you won't get stepped on.

(SHEILA *exits to the kitchen.* BRI *enters up* C *wheeling* JOE *in her invalid chair.* JOE *is ten, physically normal but for the stiffness of her legs and arms. Her legs, at this stage, are covered with a blanket. She cannot support herself properly and has to be propped wherever she is put; for the most part she lies supine. In her chair, she sits with the upper part of her body forward on the tray in front of her chair, as though asleep. Her face is pretty but vacant of expression, her voice feeble.* BRI, *who carries a small grip marked BOAC, pushes the chair* C)

BRI. There we are then, lovely. Home again. (*He moves away* RC, *puts down the grip on the sofa, then looks at Joe*) Safe and sound. You been a good girl?

JOE (*this is her closest approach to speech*) A-aaah!

BRI (*locking the invalid chair*) Really good?

JOE. Aaaah!

BRI. The lady in the bus said you'd been good. Sat by the driver, did you?

JOE. Aaaah!

BRI. There's a clever girl!

JOE. Aaaah!

BRI (*as though he understood*) Saw the Christmas trees?

JOE. Aaaah!

BRI. And the shops lit up?

JOE. Aaah!

BRI. What d'you say? (*He sits on the coffee-table*) Saw *Jesus*? Where was he, where was Jesus, you poor softy?

(SHEILA *enters and moves above the sofa to* L *of the chair*)

JOE. Aaaah!

BRI. I see. (*He moves* LC *and picks up the grip*)

SHEILA. My great big beautiful darling home at last? (*She kneels by the chair*) Got a great big beautiful kiss for Mummy? (*She kisses Joe, then moves above the chair*)

JOE. Aaaah!

SHEILA. I'm lovely, she says. (*She sits on the* R *end of the chaise*)

BRI. Mad, she says, but lovely.

SHEILA. She been a good girl, Dad? Did the lady say?

BRI. Very good, Mum. Sat by the driver.

SHEILA (*with shocked amazement*) Did you sit by the driver? Did you, lovely?

(BRI *and* SHEILA *act as parents do receiving home a child of two from the Infants' School*)

BRI. Saw the Christmas trees, Mum.

SHEILA. Did you see the Christmas trees? *What* a clever girl!

BRI. And Jesus.
SHEILA. Jesus?
BRI. Bathed in light, in the sky.
SHEILA (*to Bri; aside*) She got a screw loose, Dad?
BRI. No, Mum.
SHEILA. Seeing Jesus?
BRI. On top the Electricity Building.
SHEILA (*relieved*) Oh, yes! Thought she was off her chump for a minute, Dad.
BRI. Seeing Jesus in a dump like this? No wonder, Mum. But no, she's doing well, they say.
SHEILA. Daddy's pleased you're trying, love. What with your eleven-plus on the way.
BRI. You want to get to a decent school.
SHEILA. I don't want to be shunted into some secondary modern slum, she says . . . (*She kisses Joe again*)
BRI. Like the one where Daddy works . . .
SHEILA. Share a room with forty or fifty council-house types and blackies.
BRI. No, I've had enough of them, she says, at the Spastics' Nursery. You want to go on to the Training Centre, help to make those ball-point pens. (*He rummages in the grip*)
JOE. Aaaah!
SHEILA. I'm trying my hardest, she says.
BRI. You keep it up, my girl. (*Taking out a note*) Hallo, what's this? It's a note from Mrs Whats-it.
SHEILA. From the Nursery?
BRI. A school report, Mum. (*Reading*) "Thank you for the present for Colin's birthday." Which is Colin?
SHEILA. Little boy who had meningitis.
BRI. Never stops whimpering?
SHEILA. That's him.
BRI. Did you send him Many Happy Returns?
SHEILA. I sent a card. And a cuddly bunny.
BRI. It's the thought that counts. (*Reading*) "Quite a few of the parents remembered and the kitchen ladies made a lovely cake with seven candles and we held up Colin so he could see them burning, then we all helped him blow them out."

(*Without looking at each other*, SHEILA *and* BRI *make the "Aaaah!" sound of a cinema audience at being shown a new-born lamb*)

"The physiotherapist lady came and looked at us all today and said Josephine's shoulders show some signs of improvement. She says keep on with the exercises."
SHEILA. Do your homework like a good girl. (*Rising*) Daddy help.
BRI (*to Joe*) Mummy can't. She's going out for a bit on the side.
SHEILA. Let me call your mother. Please.

BRI (*ignoring her, rising and reading on*) Hullo, hullo, what's *this* I see? What's this? "She's had a few fits today but I think it must have been the excitement over Colin's cake." (*He moves down* R *and back, acting the cross father*)

SHEILA (*stopping the comedy and beginning to be seriously concerned*) Oh dear, now why's that, I wonder?

BRI (*to Joe, moving* C) Just you listen to me, my girl . . .

SHEILA. I thought we'd got them under control.

BRI (*to Joe*) How are you to raise yourself above the general level if you keep having fits?

SHEILA. This is the first for weeks—except an occasional petit mal.

BRI. Those council-house types down there, what d'you think they say? (*Going into a heavy village rustic act*) "She puts it on, a voice you could cut with a knife—Lady Bleedin' Muck and no mistake! But look at her, she's no better than the likes of us, just another raver."

SHEILA. Poor kid, poor blossom. (*She caresses Joe*)

BRI. Spare the rod spoil the child, Mum.

SHEILA. I don't know why they've started.

BRI. Welfare State. Life's all too easy these days—free milk, show-jumping. Physiotherapy. Singing and candles. What singing and candles did we have at her age? Air-raids and clothing coupons, and if we didn't like that, my mother used to say: "That's all you're getting, my sonner".

(JOE'S *head turns slowly from one side to the other*)

SHEILA. Hullo.

(BRI *and* SHEILA *watch silently.* JOE'S *mouth closes and she undergoes a seizure—not violent, but slow and tense, the head turning, one arm stretching out.* SHEILA *goes to Joe, touches her forehead, and puts her arm back on her lap. Then she crosses to Bri, takes the note and reads it*)

That's great, that is. Explains it.

BRI. What?

SHEILA. They're run out of anti-convulsant suspension again.

BRI. Again?

SHEILA (*reading*) "—excitement over Colin's cake. Or perhaps because we've used up all her yellow medicine."

BRI. Call themselves a day nursery.

SHEILA. How many times is this?

BRI. Why don't they keep a few spare bottles in the fridge? Nearly all the kids need it.

SHEILA. The amount they use, they should have it on draught.

(SHEILA *exits to the kitchen.* JOE'S *fit finished, she rests on the shelf*)

BRI (*excited by Sheila's suggestion*) Yes! Drawn to the nurseries and day-centres in barrels by a dirty great fleet of dray-horses. (*He acts the commentator with an awe-struck voice, as if holding a hand-mike*) And here—in the City Pharmacy—you can stand—as I'm standing now

—in the nerve-centre of this great operation of mercy—and watch the myriad craftsmen at their various chores.

(Sheila *enters with two bottles, one of pills and one of yellow medicine, and a spoon. She gives the pills to Bri*)

Sheila. Give her the phenos. (*She unlocks the chair and turns it so that Joe is facing upstage*)

Bri. Or something less trad? (*He takes two pills from the bottle and moves upstage*)

(Sheila *shakes the other bottle, moving* L *of Joe*)

Bit more in keeping with our forward-looking technological society? A central pumping station and a vast complex of underground culverts and sluice-gates.

Sheila (*to Joe*) Soon be better, my flower.

(Bri *forces Joe's jaws apart and puts the pills into her mouth*)

Bri. No, but they'll never stand for it.

Sheila. Who?

Bri. Bristol's ratepayers. Cost a fortune. One pheno.

Sheila. Here, my blossom, lovely orange. (*She spoons it in*)

Bri. Too fond of the ceremonial, the bull.

Sheila. There's a clever girl.

Bri (*holding Joe's jaw shut*) New life to dying crafts. Horse-brasses in the sun, tang of cooper's apron. (*He makes the sound effects of horse-hooves and whinnying*) Dagenham Girl Pipers.

(Sheila *stoppers the bottles*)

Sheila. And for a special treat, Mummy got her favourite ice-cream for tea.

Bri (*releases Joe's jaw*) Gone down now.

Sheila. Tell Mummy—are you wet?

(Bri *looks in the grip*)

(*Putting her hand under Joe's blanket*) Soaking.

Bri (*taking a nappy from the grip*) This nappy's dry.

Sheila (*indignantly*) Honestly! They've started *doing* that again this week. Leaving the one I send in the bag and letting her sit like Joe Egg in the damp all day. Her parts get spreathed.

Bri. Perhaps she was *dry* before the fit.

Sheila. She could hardly have gone all day without a wee.

Bri. No.

Sheila (*moving upstage and looking at her watch*) Will *you* change her? I must go and get ready.

(Bri *throws the nappy on Joe's chair-shelf and takes the bottles from Sheila*)

If she's spreathed, there's ointment in the cupboard.

(BRI *nods, with a cheesy smile*)

And if I were you, I should put her on the kitchen floor to change her.

BRI (*putting the bottles and spoon in the grip and hooking it on the chair*) I'm not the new nannie.

SHEILA (*after a pause*) No. Course not, but . . .

BRI (*wheeling Joe* R) I've done it before. Once or twice. In the last ten years.

(BRI *exits up* R, *wheeling* JOE)

SHEILA. Bri.

(BRI *enters*)

(*Moving above the sofa to Bri*) Shall I call your mother?

BRI. What for?

SHEILA. So we can go out.

BRI. Tuesday night there's nowhere much to go. The zoo's shut. There's a Western at the Gaumont.

SHEILA. Come and see the rehearsal.

(BRI *and* SHEILA *hold each other*)

Get drunk if you like. But not too drunk to bring me home and have me.

BRI (*pointing towards Joe*) Pas devant . . .

SHEILA. What?

BRI. Pas devant l'enfant.

SHEILA. Aitch-ay-vee-ee me. Seriously. Shall I?

(BRI *kisses her, buries his face in her hair, then emerges*)

BRI. Hey, listen! What's it like with Freddie?

(SHEILA *stiffens, then struggles to break free*)

(*Holding her*) No, come on, you've told me about the others. Not all, of course—

SHEILA. Let go . . .

BRI. —but a sampling—a cross-section—

SHEILA. I shall bite.

BRI. —the ones that because of some exceptional feature stand out from the crowd.

SHEILA. They were all before I met you.

BRI. But Freddie's *now*.

SHEILA. Let go.

BRI. What's his speciality?

SHEILA. Even if he wanted to—which he doesn't—

BRI. You must think I'm soft.

SHEILA. —Freddie would run a mile from a breath of scandal, you know that!

BRI. No, but I mean—what's his gimmick?

SHEILA. Come and ask him.

BRI. For instance—

SHEILA. Why don't you?

BRI. —those four Americans, you said, made you . . .

SHEILA. What? Where d'you get that?

BRI. What?

SHEILA. Four Americans.

BRI. Wrong?

SHEILA. Two Americans.

BRI. Oh.

SHEILA (*breaking from Bri to below the sofa*) One Canadian.

BRI (*following her*) Ah. Then the Welshman—the stoker . . .

SHEILA. He wasn't a stoker. He was a policeman.

BRI. Oh, yes. He was shocked because you used bad words in a posh accent. But when it came to getting off your frock, he was so ravenous he tore it.

SHEILA (*sitting on the sofa*, R) I wish I'd never told you anything. You said we should be *honest*. You told me all about yours first.

BRI (*sitting beside her; nodding*) All three. That took an hour. Then for the next few weeks you made a short-list.

SHEILA. You *made* me.

BRI. You must have enjoyed those fellows at the time.

SHEILA. No!

BRI. One or two.

SHEILA. I've told you.

BRI. Why go on with it then?

SHEILA. Once you get to a certain stage with a man, it's hard to say no.

BRI. Most women manage it. With *me*, at any rate. *Three* out of God knows how many tens of thousands I tried . . .

SHEILA. They didn't know a good thing when they saw it.

BRI. That's true.

SHEILA. You were the only one who gave *me* any pleasure.

BRI. When you first told me that I was knocked out. I walked round for days feeling like a phallic symbol. (*Rising*) She'll stick with me, I thought happily, because I've got magic super-zoom with added cold-start.

SHEILA. You have, yes.

BRI. Till Freddie . . .

SHEILA. O ye Gods.

BRI. Of all people! (*He sits again*)

SHEILA. He's never been near me.

BRI. I think we should still be honest. Even about him.

SHEILA. He leaves me cold.

BRI. And yet you'd rather spend the evening with him than with me.

SHEILA. You pushed me into this drama lark. You said I should get out . . .

BRI. What's his speciality? His forté? Does he keep his mac on?

(SHEILA *faces him for several seconds. Then she rises and exits up* C. BRI *shrugs, then sighs.* JOE *cries off*)

All right, lovely, Daddy's here.

(BRI *rises, goes to the kitchen and returns wheeling* JOE. *He moves her down* R *of the sofa*)

Did it hurt? Did you bump your nose? (*He props Joe up*) Better?

(JOE *sneezes*)

Bless you. You look pale, Joe. Is it those nasty fits? Never mind. (*He fondles Joe's hand*) Lovely soft hands you've got. Like silk. Lady's hands. *They've* never done rough work. (*Crouching by the chair*) Now. Mum's gone to take her part. Practice her acting. So we'll have a bit of a chinwag round the oil heater. Chew the fat, watch the jumping. (*He moves to the television* L *and picks up the* 'Radio Times') I expect there's jumping, there usually is. (*Looking in the paper*) Come Dancing. No, no jumping. (*Moving back to Joe*) There's a film about an eminent surgeon and his fight against injustice in London's East End. (*Showing Joe*) I know you can't resist a doctor. (*Aside, to the audience*) When you think what they did to her! (*Back to Joe, sitting on the couch*) But before that, Daddy get her a lovely tea. Joe and Daddy have a lovely tea then Joe have a nice hot bath? Play with her ducks? Hear that noise? That's Mummy in the bedroom. Probably taken her dress off now. Might be putting her stockings on. Even changing entirely. Every stitch. Naked, looking at herself in the glass, thinking have I kept my figure? (*He pauses, dwelling on the image*) But I'm not running up those stairs three at a time and falling into the bedroom and cringing on the carpet begging her not to go. No fear! I've done all I can without total loss of dignity. I might have known once I got her started on amateur theatricals she'd turn up at every bloody practice. Terrible sense of duty, your mum. (*He looks at Joe lolling in her chair*) What am I doing, talking to you? (*He rises, moves down* C *and talks to the audience*) Might as well be talking to a wall. (*Like a front-cloth comic*) No, but she is a wonderful woman, my wife. That girl upstairs. In the bedroom—(*moving down* L)—off in the wings (*returning* C)—wherever she is. That is no actress, that is my wife. No, seriously. (*He drops his act and continues as himself*) A truly integrated person. Very rare, that is, as you know. Give you an example: she's disturbed by anything, she's not just mentally upset about it, not only miserable, no she actually grows *ill*. Boils, back-ache, vomiting. Not pretence. Real sickness. She works as a whole, not in parts. Unlike me, for instance, I'm Instant Man. Get one for Christmas, endless fun. I'm made up as I go along from old lengths of string, fag-ends—magazine cuttings, film-clips—all stuck together with wodges of last week's school dinner. What I mean, *she* couldn't pretend a passion she doesn't feel. Whereas I can't sustain a passion to the end of the sentence. I start to cry—aaaoooow! Then I think, are you mad? Who do you think you are, God? And things go clang and wheels fall off and people get hurt—terrible. You must have felt like this—catching yourself in the mirror hamming away. Or somebody says: "My wife's just been run over", and you want to burst out laughing. Well, you may say, why not—if that's the way you feel? But other people don't like it. So I pretend. You saw me pretend with Sheila. I try to guess which emotions appeal to her and then I sink my teeth in. I don't let go until they're bone-dry. Like with Joe there—(*waving at her*)—all right, are you? Good. I felt all doomy at first but—well—ten years! I just go through the motions now. Sheila—how shall I put it in a way that will prevent a sudden stampede to the exit-doors? Sheila—embraces all living things. She really does. She's simple, so simple she's bound to win in the end. She's a sane enough person to be able to embrace all living creatures. She sits there embracing all live things. I get my hug somewhere between the budgerigar and the stick-insect. Which is the reason for all this smutty talk. Calling attention to myself to make sure I get more than my share. Otherwise I'd have to settle for eyes-front-hands-on-heads and a therapeutic bash once in a blue moon. And I'm too young to die, I tell you!

Joe. Aaaah!

Bri (*moving to Joe*) What's that, lovely? What's that, crackpot?

Joe. Aaaah!

Bri. Language. You think this is language! I'll introduce you to Scanlon. He'll let you hear some language. (*Aside*) What a madam! Well. Let's see what she's left you for tea. Go and get your tea, change your nappy. (*He pushes Joe's chair to the kitchen. Going out, he struggles with the cats*) Get back, you flea-bitten whores! Get back!

(Bri *exits with* Joe, *closing the door behind him. There is a pause of at least five seconds then* Sheila *enters up* c. *She has changed into a dress and is carrying a small make-up bag. She moves down* c)

Sheila. One of these days I'll hit him. Honestly. (*She attends to her make-up, looking at the audience*) He thinks because he throws a tantrum I'm going to stay home comforting him and miss the rehearsal and let them all down. He thinks he's only got to cry to get all he wants. I blame his mother. She gave him the kind of suffocating love that makes him think the world revolved around him, but because he's too intelligent to believe it really, he gets into these paddies and depressions. And when he's in one of those, he'll do anything to draw attention to himself. That spider on his face—you saw that. (*She goes down* l, *picks up the chair, returns* c *and sits*) And all this stuff about Freddie. And yet it was Brian made me join these amateurs in the first place; he said I needed to get out more, have a rest from Joe. But she's no trouble. It's Brian. I don't know which is the greatest baby. Watching somebody as limited as Joe over ten years, I've begun to feel she's only one kind of cripple. Everybody's damaged in some way. There's a limit to what we can do. Brian, for instance, he goes so far—and hits the ceiling. Just can't fly any higher. Then he drops to the floor and we get self-pity again—despair. I'm sure, though, if he could go further—he could be a marvellous painter. That's another reason I said I'd join the amateurs: the thought that he'd be forced to go upstairs several nights a week and actually put paint on canvas. And even if he *isn't* any good, he seems to need some work he can be proud of. Something to take his mind off his jealousy of anyone or anything I take to—relatives, friends, pets—even pot-plants. I'm sure it's because they take up time he thinks I could be devoting to him. And Joe, of course, Joe, most of all, poor love. (*She rises, a thought bringing her back*) Look, you mustn't assume I feel like this in the ordinary way. And even when I *am* a bit down, I shouldn't normally talk about it to a lot of complete strangers. (*She goes to the television table and puts her make-up bag down*) But all this childish temper over Freddie—this showing-off—it's more than I can stand. (*She returns to the chair and sits*) It makes me boil, honestly! Wouldn't you feel the same? That's why I'm telling you all this. A lot of total strangers. But wouldn't it make *you* boil? Honestly! A grown man jealous of poor Joe . . .

(SHEILA *breaks off as* BRI *enters* R *and moves down to her*)

BRI. What are you telling them?

SHEILA. What?

BRI. I heard you talking.

(SHEILA *picks thread from her clothes*)

I heard you mention Joe.

(SHEILA *does not answer*)

(*To the audience*) Sheila's got a theory about Joe's birth. She doesn't blame the doctors. She blames herself.

SHEILA. I don't say that. I say it wasn't *entirely* the doctors.

BRI (*nodding*) It was because she choked it back.

SHEILA. It was partly that.

BRI. Because she's slept around.

SHEILA. I think it was partly because I'd been promiscuous, yes, and my subconscious was making me shrink or withdraw from motherhood, all right!

(*There is a pause.* BRI *looks away.* SHEILA *goes on titivating*)

BRI. That vicar said it was the devil's doing. Why don't you believe *that*? It's about as brilliant.

SHEILA (*shrugging*) It comes down in the end to what you believe.

BRI (*moving nearer to Sheila*) I'll tell you what I believe.

SHEILA. I *know* what you believe.

BRI (*pointing at the audience*) They don't. (*To the audience*) I believe the doctor botched it. There was no other cause. (*To Sheila*) That specialist said as much, he said it had nothing at all to do with the way you'd lived or whether there was a nut in the family—or what kind of fags you smoked . . .

SHEILA. He didn't say the doctor did it either.

BRI (*after a pause; looking at her*) No. You've got a good point there. He didn't mention that, quite true. He didn't say: "Yes, he's a shoddy midwife, my colleague, always was, I'll see he gets struck off the register." Very true. Quite spoils my argument, that.

SHEILA (*rising and moving down* L) Oh, you're so *clever*!'

BRI. He'd only say for certain that it was a chance in a million it could happen again.

SHEILA. Mmm. We haven't had an opportunity yet to check on that.

(*They both pause*)

BRI. It's due to this of course that Joe lives at home with us.

SHEILA (*moving towards* C) She's our daughter.

BRI (*to the audience*) She was on the way before we married. That feeds the furnace of guilt.

SHEILA (*moving further* C) No need to tell them everything.

BRI. It was a white wedding.

SHEILA. For my Dad's sake. He was a bellringer and always looked forward to the day he'd lead the peal as I left the church. You said you didn't mind.

BRI. I didn't. At the reception afterwards the ringers were the only people worth talking to. All twisted and crippled. Picture them bouncing up and down at the end of their ropes. (*He moves to Sheila and tries a guess at it*)

SHEILA. We might have taken them for an omen. The baby came six months later. I'd done my exercises and read the ante-natal books—mostly the ones that made it seem as simple as having a tooth filled.

BRI. But more spiritual. (*He sits in Sheila's chair*)

SHEILA. Oh yes, a lot about you sitting by the bed holding my hand and looking sincere.

BRI (*doing this*) Giving the lead with shallow breathing. (*He acts shallow breathing also*)

SHEILA. Down, Rover. (*To the audience*) I don't know whether any of you are like me, but I half-expected to hear snatches of the Hallelujah Chorus.

BRI (*rising and moving* R *a little; to the audience*) How long do *your* labours last? Two, three hours? A day? Dilettantes! (*Pointing at Sheila*) Five days!

SHEILA. Yes. From the first pang to the last groan. Five days.

BRI. You'll all be saying: "He should have *done* something", but I didn't *know* at the time. You don't, do you?

SHEILA. You know now.

BRI. Oh, yeah. It was all good experience.

SHEILA (*to the audience*) This doctor kept on drugging me.

Bri. You were stoned.

Sheila. I couldn't remember the exercises.

Bri. Couldn't even tell me. Just kept crying.

Sheila (*explaining*) I couldn't make anyone understand! I couldn't salivate or swallow so I stayed hungry—also I kept hoping you'd be there when I opened my eyes, but it was always the midwife or your mother.

Bri. Not always.

Sheila. Nearly always. You were getting drunk outside.

Bri. What else could I do?

Sheila (*to the audience*) My speech faculties seemed to have gone, so I couldn't tell them to stop drugging me so that I could manage the birth.

(*For the rest of the act*, Sheila *and* Bri *hold a dialogue with each other and the audience. No further indication is given, unless essential to the sense*)

Bri. Then the G.P. would pop in to see me with his boyish grin—"Tell the truth I've got the feeling this young shaver's none too keen to join us." And I'd say: "All this trouble getting out and he'll spend the rest of his life trying to get back in." And we'd all kill ourselves at that and have another Scotch.

Sheila. You never thought it was going on too long?

Bri. Yes, but you leave it to them, don't you? My mum taught me to believe in doctors and during the labour she set an example of quiet faith.

Sheila. And afterwards—when Joe was ill—she said she knew all along it was lasting too long.

Bri. She always knows afterwards.

Sheila. The pain was shocking but the worst was not being able to speak.

Bri. By the last day I thought she was going to die. And—I've never told you this, love . . . (*He moves to the chair and puts his foot on it*) Though not normally a religious man—

(Sheila *moves in to the chair*)

—for everyday purposes making the usual genuflections to Esso Petroleum and M.G.M.—I don't mind admitting it, I got down on my knees and prayed.

Sheila. Did you really?

Bri. Yes.

Sheila. Not another joke?

Bri (*taking her hand*) No, honestly. I prayed to God. I said: "God, I've only just found her. The baby doesn't matter. If it's a question of a swop . . ."

Sheila. Aaaah!

Bri. Then I found I was so drunk I could hardly get to my feet again.

SHEILA (*moving* L *a little*) But never mind, your prayer was answered.

BRI (*moving* R *a little*) Yes, he heard all right. (*To the audience*) I see him as a sort of manic depressive rugby-footballer, and I'm the ball.

SHEILA. By the time the damage was done, they took me to hospital. The next thing I knew, they handed me this hairless yellow baby with forcep-scars all over her scalp. She was gorgeous. By the time I got her home, the scars and jaundice were gone and she was in working order. You had a cold.

BRI (*moving upstage*) That's right, yes.

SHEILA. I had to look after you. It was better than having you turn up every day moaning and sniffling.

BRI (*returning downstage*) More than a cold, 'flu. A delayed action I think it must have been. I was quite poorly.

(SHEILA *smiles, then turns to the audience*)

SHEILA. Soon I began to notice these funny turns. We asked our friends who'd had babies but they said it was most likely wind. So in the end we took her to our new G.P.

(*The upstage part of the set dims to semi-darkness.* BRI *fetches a tubular cushion, the size and shape of a swaddled baby, from the chaise.* SHEILA *wheels the trolley down* C, *puts the teapot and other things on the bottom shelf, spreads the cloth over the top shelf, and turns the trolley crosswise to the footlights. She then moves below* R *of the trolley.* BRI *moves* L *of Sheila and gives her the cushion, which she nurses*)

BRI. Baby. (*Pointing to himself*) Doctor. Nice, bone-headed.

(*In the sketches which follow,* BRI *plays the funny men and* SHEILA *herself. They do it as they might repeat the dialogue from a favourite film. Sometimes they improvise, surprising or "corpsing" each other.* SHEILA *moves* R *and sits on the chair down* R. BRI *moves* L *and mimes opening a door*)

Bye-bye, Mrs—um—you rub that in you'll soon be as right as rain. (*He mimes closing the door, returns* C *and shouts*) Next, please!

(SHEILA *rises and moves* R *of the trolley.* BRI *bends over, writing and putting away the last patient's card*)

Evening, Mister—um—feeling any better?

SHEILA. It's morning, doctor. (*To the audience*) Not very reassuring.

BRI (*rising and moving* L, *taking out a card*) Course it is.

SHEILA. And I've never been before.

BRI. No?

SHEILA. We're new to the district.

BRI (*moving to Sheila*) What seems to be the trouble?

SHEILA. I don't really know. Funny turns. Face-making.

BRI. Say "aaah!"

SHEILA. Not me. The baby.

BRI (*looking at the cushion*) Nothing much wrong with this little laddie.

SHEILA. Lassie.

BRI. Lassie. Funny turns, you say. How would you describe them?

SHEILA. Frightening.

BRI. No, I meant, what form do they take?

SHEILA. Blinking with her eyes, working with her tongue, shaking her head, then going all limp.

BRI (*tickling the baby, talking to it*) Funny turns indeed at your age! Saucy beggar. We are not amused.

SHEILA. But what d'you think it is?

BRI. Wind.

SHEILA. That's what our friends said.

BRI. Always wise to get a second opinion. Have you tried Gripe Water?

SHEILA. Yes, of course.

BRI. My old mother used to swear by it. Cure anything, she used to say. Well, let's see what we can find in here. (*He moves* L *a little and mimes opening a drawer, finding medicine and reading the label. Returning to Sheila*) Ah yes, this'll put a stop to it. Came in the post this morning. The makers praise it very highly.

SHEILA. Doctor—I wish you could *see* one of these turns.

BRI. Oh, I've seen them, dear. Got three great monsters of my own.

SHEILA. I am sorry.

BRI. What?

SHEILA. All your children being—um . . .

BRI. No, I mean great thriving brutes. Not monsters, no. Silly girl. Your first, is it?

SHEILA. What?

BRI. First baby?

SHEILA. Yes.

BRI. Well, dear, it's like this. You're throwing an awful lot of gubbins down the old cake-hole there. It's like running in a new car. Till all the tappets and contact breakers get adjusted to the absolute thou, you take it easy, give 'em a chance. Same with these chaps. (*He tickles the cushion, then looks again at the medicine*) Let's see. Three times daily after meals. How often are you feeding?

SHEILA. Every four hours.

BRI. Four into twenty-four goes . . .

SHEILA. Six.

BRI. Jolly good. Six times a day.

SHEILA. Look. This may be one now.

(SHEILA *and* BRI *watch the cushion for ten seconds.* BRI *looks at his watch*)

No.

BRI. I've got a waiting-room full of people, dear. (*Leading Sheila* L) You try her with this and come back if there's no improvement in—say—a week. Make sure you wind her well. And don't fret. They're hardy little devils, you know. Bye-bye, Mrs—um . . . (*He mimes seeing her out and shutting the door*)

(SHEILA *immediately crosses* R *below the chaise and sits down* R *as before*)

Three days later. (*He moves down* R *and mimes opening the door*) Next please. (*He returns to the chair* C)

(SHEILA *comes back at once with the cushion*)

Hullo, Mrs—um . . .
SHEILA (*urgently*) Doctor . . .
BRI (*moving* L *to the "cupboard"*) Sit down, please.
SHEILA (*sitting* C) But this child . . .
BRI. Just a minute, I'll get your card. (*He looks at a "card"*) Didn't I say come back in a week? (*Moving to her*) Why so soon?
SHEILA. She's gone into a coma.
BRI. D'you try the medicine?
SHEILA. She won't take anything. She hasn't fed for two days.

(BRI *looks at the cushion, listens to it, claps hands by it, finally shakes it like a piggy-bank*)

BRI (*as much as to say "so far, so good"*) Ah—ha! Mm—hm. (*He goes humming to the "table"* L *and mimes telephoning*) Get me the Children's Hospital—quick!

(SHEILA *rises*)

No need for alarm, dear, just a routine enquiry.

(SHEILA *sits*)

Your husband with you?
SHEILA. In the waiting-room. Is she . . .?
BRI (*into the "telephone"*) Look—I'd like you to take a shufti at a baby—uh—girl?
SHEILA. Yes.
BRI. Baby girl—off her chow and failing to respond to any stimuli whatever. (*To Sheila*) Got a car?
SHEILA. No.
BRI. Hullo? No car. Any chance of an ambulance? . . . Understood. Thank you. 'Bye. (*He puts down the "telephone" and returns to Sheila*)
SHEILA (*rising*) There's something seriously wrong, isn't there?
BRI. Don't start worrying, dear. Look at it this way. You know when you get a starter-motor jammed? Seems serious at the time, but put it in second gear and rock the whole shoot back and forth, she's soon as right as rain.

SHEILA. We haven't got a car, I . . .

BRI. What I want you to do—you know the kiddies' hospital?

(SHEILA *nods*)

(*Leading her* L) You and your old man go along there—not forgetting to take the baby—you catch a bus from the end of the street. And—nil desperandum. 'Bye, Mrs—um. (*He sees her to the "door", opens it and pushes her through. He is about to close it again when he remembers something and shouts after her*) Thirty-two.

SHEILA (*returning*) What?

BRI. The bus. Number thirty-two.

SHEILA. Oh. (*She puts the cushion on the chaise and crosses to down* R)

BRI (*closing the "door", taking out his handkerchief and mopping his brow*) Strewth. (*He moves upstage*)

SHEILA (*turning to the audience*) On the bus I said to Brian: "I've got a feeling we shan't bring her back." But, as you know, we did. Eventually.

BRI (*moving downstage*) Every cloud has a jet-black lining.

SHEILA. I stayed in hospital with her for a few weeks, then left her there having tests and came home to look after Brian, who'd contracted impetigo. It was painful.

BRI. Yes, it was.

SHEILA. It was painful not feeding, so in the end a woman from the clinic drew it off with a sort of glass motor-horn. A few weeks later they called me to collect Joe from hospital, by which time we'd gathered she wasn't ever going to amount to much.

(BRI *goes to the chaise for the cushion and puts it on the trolley, standing upstage of it*)

But I was determined to know the best we could expect. And the worst. The pediatrician was German—or Viennese, I'm not sure which.

(*For the following sketch,* BRI *uses a music-hall German accent*)

BRI. Vell, mattam, zis baby off yours has now been soroughly tested and ve need ze bets razzer battly so it's better you take her home. I sink I can promise she von't be any trouble. Keep her vell sedated you'll hartly know she's zere. (*He moves upstage*)

SHEILA (*moving* L *above the trolley*) But, doctor . . .

BRI (*returning downstage reluctantly*) Ja?

SHEILA. Can't you tell me the results?

BRI. Results?

SHEILA. Of the tests.

BRI. Vitch vones? Zere vere so many. (*He gives a slight laugh, and lists on his fingers*) Electro-encephalograph, scree-dimensional eggs-ray, blood urine and stool analyses, zis business vis needles in ze fontanelle . . .

SHEILA. Is that why her hair's been shaved off?

Bri. Vell of course . . .

Sheila. She'd only just begun to grow it. And did the needles make that scar on her head?

Bri. Scar?

Sheila (*pointing*) There.

Bri. Ach, nein. Zis vos a liddly biopsy to take a sample of her brain tissue.

Sheila. That's a relief. (*She smiles quickly*) I thought at first you'd bored a hole in her skull to let the devil out.

(Bri *moves down* L *and consults with his "assistant"*)

Bri. Sounds gut. Did you try it? . . . Ah! (*To Sheila*) My colleague says ve don't do zat any more. (*He shrugs*) Pity! Vell—if you eggscuse me . . . (*He moves below the trolley and upstage*)

Sheila. But doctor—doctor . . .

Bri (*returning*) Donner und blitzen!

Sheila. What can she *do*?

Bri. Do? She can't do nozzing at all.

Sheila. Will she ever?

Bri. Mattam, let me try and tell you vot your daughter iss like. Do you know vot I mean ven I say your daughter vos a wegetable?

(Sheila *thinks for a moment, then gets it and smiles*)

Sheila. Yes! You mean "Your daughter was a vegetable."

Bri. Ach himmel! Still is, still *is*, always vill be! I have trouble vis Englisch werbs.

Sheila. But—when people say to me what kind of cripple is your child, shall I say—she's a wege- a *v*egetable?

Bri. You vont a vord for her? (*He shrugs*) You can say she iss a spastic vis a damaged cerebral cortex, multiplegic, epileptic, but vis no organic malformation of ze brain.

Sheila. That *is* a long word.

Bri (*gaily*) Which iss vy I prefer wegetable.

Sheila. *V*egetable.

Bri. *V*egetable.

Sheila. But why? If her brain's physically sound, why doesn't it work?

(Bri *sighs, looks at her, thinks*)

Bri (*moving* L *of her*) Good question. Imagine a svitchboard. A telephone svitchboard, ja?

Sheila (*sitting in the chair* C) I worked as a switchboard operator once.

Bri. Wunderbar! Vell. Imagine you're zitting zere now, facing ze board, so?

Sheila. Right.

Bri. Some lines tied up, some vaiting to be used. Suddenly brr-brr, brr-brr . . .

SHEILA. Incoming call?
BRI. Exactly. You plug in.

(SHEILA *mimes the switchboard, assuming a bright telephone voice*)

SHEILA. Universal Shafting.
BRI (*coming out of character*) What?
SHEILA. That was the firm I worked for.
BRI (*laughing*) You've never put that in before.
SHEILA (*shrugging*) I thought I would this time.
BRI. Universal Shafting? (*He laughs*)

(SHEILA *stares coldly.* BRI *clears his throat and resumes as the doctor*)

But at zat moment anozzer incoming call—and you panic and plug him into ze first von and leave zem talking to each ozzer and you answer an extension and he asks for the railway station but you put him on to ze cricket results and zey all start buzzing and flashing—and it's too much, you flip your lid and pull out all the lines. Kaputt! Now zere's your epileptic fit. Grand or Petit Mal, according to ze stress, ze number of calls. (*He moves a little upstage*) All right? (*Makes to go again*)

SHEILA. But, doctor, doctor . . .
BRI (*looks at his watch*) Gott in himmel! I'm wery busy man, Missis—um . . .
SHEILA. I know you must be . . .
BRI. Yours isn't ze only piecan in ze country . . .
SHEILA. I know . . .
BRI (*as himself, to audience*) There's one born every eight hours, did you know that?
SHEILA. No, I didn't. Is that true?
BRI. Oh, ja, ja. Not all as bad as zees case, of course . . .
SHEILA. Isn't there anything at all we can do?
BRI. But jawohl! You must feed her, voshh her nappies, keep her varm. Just like any ozzer mozzer.
SHEILA. But for how long?
BRI. Who can tell, Anysing can happen, you know zat. Diphtheria, pneumonia—vooping cough—Colorado beetle.

(SHEILA *laughs, they come out of character*)

SHEILA. Oh, that's terrible. Colorado beetle.
BRI. I only just thought of that.
SHEILA. It's terrible.
BRI (*as himself*) So—what happened then? We brought her home.
SHEILA. And the hospital passed the can back to our local G.P.
BRI. The piecan.
SHEILA. He had to supply phenobarbitone and keep us happy. He used to come once a week to explain her fits. In layman's terms.
BRI. You didn't find out much?
SHEILA. About fits, no, but I learnt a lot about distributors and contact breakers.

BRI. Or what happens at a cross-roads when the traffic lights fail.
SHEILA. But the time came when I asked him whose fault it was.
BRI. Which is when he suggested the Vicar might call.
SHEILA. Yes. Nice Vicar. Sensitive. So concerned and upset at the sight of Joe—the fits were unusually bad that day—so we left her in the bedroom and had our chat in another room.

(*There is quite a long pause while they prepare themselves for the next scene. The mood changes slightly.* BRI *allows* SHEILA *to take the initiative and plays the Vicar quietly, even seriously, to begin with.* BRI *takes the cushion and cloth from the trolley, puts them on the chaise, and moves up* C. SHEILA *brings the chair from down* R *to* R *of the trolley and moves up* C. *They meet.* BRI *takes out a pipe and they both move downstage to above the trolley*)

Here we are. Do take a pew.

(BRI, *as the Vicar, laughs*)

Oh! (*She laughs also*)

(*They both sit and mime drinking tea*)

BRI. She's a beautiful child.
SHEILA. Yes, isn't she?
BRI. It's tragic. Tell me—when you first—knew there was nothing to be done, how did you feel?
SHEILA. Well, of course, you find out gradually, not all at once. But there is a point when you finally accept it. And that's—(*shaking her head*)—oh, very nasty. You think "why me?" I don't know about the other mothers but *I* kept saying "Why me, why us?" all day long. Then you get tired of that and you say "Why not me?"
BRI. Indeed. You learn humility. You recognize that we are surely in a vale of tears and you are no exception.
SHEILA. I recognized that I was worse. I'd been promiscuous, you see. All kinds of men. It seemed to me I was responsible for Joe, being punished.
BRI. No, no.
SHEILA. No, I don't mean that either. I held the baby back. Out of guilt.
BRI. Really, my dear, you mustn't believe this. Plenty of women who've slept around afterwards become splendid mothers. Premarital intercourse is no longer considered a serious obstacle to being taken into the fold.
SHEILA. No?
BRI. Haven't you read our publications lately? You should. The good old C. of E. is nowadays a far more swinging scene that you seem to suppose.
SHEILA. I see.
BRI. Oh surely. Where the action is.
SHEILA. I've never committed adultery.

BRI. There you are! That's splendid—fabulous! Crazy! Tell me, what was your husband's reaction to the child?

SHEILA. He used to say: "Think of something worse," And of course that's easy. Joe could have grown older and developed into a real person before it happened. Or she could have been a very *intelligent* spastic without the use of her limbs. Which is worse, I think, than being a kind-of living parsnip.

BRI. Quite. You count your blessings.

SHEILA. Yes.

BRI. And that gives you fortitude.

SHEILA. No, but it's something to do. When you're up against a—disaster of this kind—an Act of God—

(BRI *clears his throat*)

—it's so *numbing* you feel you must make some sense of it—otherwise you'd . . .

BRI. Give up hope?

SHEILA. Yes. My husband doesn't feel the need to make sense of anything. He lives with despair.

BRI (*rising and coming out of character*) Did you tell him that?

SHEILA. Why not?

BRI. Bit saucy.

SHEILA. Well, don't you?

BRI (*sitting again*) Can't argue now.

SHEILA (*resuming the scene*) He says I shouldn't look for explanations.

BRI. He doesn't believe in God?

SHEILA. His own kind of God. A manic-depressive rugby footballer.

BRI. It's a start. A basis for argument. (*He smiles*)

SHEILA. He doesn't like me praying.

BRI. You have been praying?

SHEILA. What else can I do? I look at that flawless little body, those glorious eyes, and I pray for some miracle to—get her started. It seems, if we only knew the key or the combination, we could get her moving. D'you think the story of the Sleeping Beauty was about a spastic?

BRI (*rising and moving* L) Who can say indeed? (*He moves back* LC) My dear, your child's sickness doesn't please God.

SHEILA. No. Why does he allow it then?

BRI. How can we know?

SHEILA. Then how can you know it doesn't please him?

BRI. We don't know. Only guess. It may be disease and infirmity are due to the misuse of the freedom he gave us. Perhaps they exist as a stimulus to research.

SHEILA. Research?

BRI. Against infirmity and disease.

SHEILA. But if he didn't permit disease and infirmity we shouldn't need research.

Bri. But he does, so we do. (*He sits again*)

(Sheila *sighs, shaking her head*)

My dear the Devil is busy day and night. God does his best, but we don't help him much. Now and then some innocent bystander blunders into the cross-fire between good and evil and . . . (*He makes gunfire noises, ricochet-sounds, falls elaborately, clutching his chest, then recovers*)

(Sheila *watches calmly*)

Or—if you can imagine a poisonous blight that settles on an orchard of many different varieties of tree . . .

Sheila. No, please, no more parables. I've had so many from the doctor.

Bri. But how can I explain without imagery of . . .

Sheila. I misled you. I don't want explanations. I've asked the people who should have been able to explain and they couldn't.

Bri. What do you want?

Sheila. Magic.

Bri. I was just coming to that. Once or twice, over the years, we have had in this parish children like your daughter.

Sheila. Just as bad?

Bri. Oh yes, I'm sure, quite as bad. Now for those poor innocents I did the Laying on of Hands.

Sheila. What is that?

Bri. A simple ceremony in your own home. A few prayers, a hymn or two, a blessing, an imposition of hands. Nothing flashy.

Sheila. Who'd be there?

Bri. You, your husband, anyone you chose.

Sheila. My husband?

Bri. Yes. And it sounds as though he needs instruction. His prayers would hardly help us if addressed to a manic-depressive rugby footballer.

Sheila. No.

Bri. God might feel affronted.

Sheila. Yes.

Bri. He's only human, after all. No, He's not, how silly of me!

Sheila. Perhaps you could have a word with him. Over a pint.

Bri. Ah, with your husband, yes. Not that there's anything wrong with rugby. Scrum-half myself for years. Just that I feel one shouldn't make a religion of it.

Sheila. With the other children—did you have any luck? Did God—you know . . .?

Bri. There was one boy—no better than Joe—made such rapid recovery after I'd done the Laying on a few times—the medicos confessed themselves bewildered. He's twelve now, and this spring he was runner-up in the South-West Area Tap-Dancing Championships.

SHEILA. How fantastic.

(BRI *rises and begins dancing and singing*)

BRI. Happy Feet, I've got those Happy Feet,
Give me a lowdown beat . . .

SHEILA. D'you really think you could—work a miracle?

BRI (*sitting*) Not me, my dear. If a miracle happens, it's only *through* me. But remember Jairus' daughter. "Damsel, I say unto thee, arise." Who knows? Perhaps in a few years' time we shall see little Joe—(*He dances and sings again*)

Animal crackers in my soup
Lions and tigers loop the loop . . .

SHEILA (*rising and moving* R; *breaking out of the sketch*) But you wouldn't do it!

(BRI *drops his Vicar imitation*)

He was a good man, kind and sincere.

BRI (*sitting*) He was, yes.

SHEILA. And that boy was cured.

BRI. Certainly improved. And yes he was the runner-up in the Southwestareatapdancingchampionships. *But*. He never *had* been as bad as Joe.

SHEILA. I don't care . . .

BRI. I looked into it . . .

SHEILA. You shouldn't have.

BRI. I spoke to people . . .

SHEILA. Where's the harm? What else did we have?

BRI. Nothing.

SHEILA. Well!

BRI (*rising and moving* L) I'd rather have nothing than a lot of lies. (*He returns* C)

SHEILA. You're unusual.

BRI. First he'd have done it for us, then he'd have got a few of his mates in to give the prayers more Whoosh! More POW! And before long he'd have had us doing it in church gloated over by all those death-watch beetles like the victims of a disaster.

SHEILA. It might have worked. He might have magicked her.

BRI. I'm sure it was best to stop it then than later on—after he'd raised your hopes. Sheila . . .

(SHEILA *looks at him and smiles*)

(*Moving to her*) Anyway. If the vicar had got her moving, she'd only have had one personality. As it is, we've given her dozens over the years.

SHEILA (*to the audience*) As soon as we were admitted to the free-masonry of spastics parents, we saw she had even less character than the other children. So we began to make them for her.

BRI. Some never really suited.

Sheila. No. Like the concert pianist dying of t.b.

Bri. Nor the girl who was tragically in love with a darkie against her parents' wishes.

Sheila. That was based on "Would you let your daughter marry one?"

Bri. I used to like the drunken bag who threw bottles at us if we didn't fetch her gin and pipe-tobacco.

Sheila. But they were all too active. The facial expression wasn't right.

Bri. The one that's stuck is the coach-tour lady—powder-pink felt hat, white gloves, Cuban heel shoes, swagger-coat . . .

Sheila. And seasick pills in her handbag in case there's a lot of twisting and turning.

Bri. She hates council houses and foreigners . . .

Sheila. Loves the Queen . . .

Bri. And Jesus. She sees him as an eccentric English gentleman. Sort of Lawrence of Arabia.

Sheila. Very disapproving of pleasure.

Bri. Not *all* pleasure. A nice Julie Andrews film with tea after . . .

Sheila. Tea in the Odeon café . . .

Bri. Nothing nicer. Which reminds me. I'm supposed to be giving her tea. In this play we started doing. (*He looks at his watch*)

Shelia. We got side-tracked.

Bri (*taking the trolley and wheeling it towards the kitchen door*) She'll have something to say to me. She'll have me on the carpet. "Nice thing leaving the table before you've finished eating, leaving me stuck here like Joe Egg . . .

(Bri *exits up* R *with the trolley.* Sheila *watches him out of sight*)

Sheila (*taking the* R *chair down* R) I join in these jokes to please him. If it helps him live with her, I can't see the harm, can you? He hasn't any faith she's ever going to improve. Where I have, you see. I believe, even if she *showed* improvement, Bri wouldn't notice. He's dense about faith—(*taking the* L *chair down* L)—faith isn't believing in fairy-tales, it's being in a receptive frame of mind. I'm always on the look-out for some sign. (*She looks up* R *to make sure Bri is not coming*) One day when she was—what?—about twelve months old, I suppose, she was lying on the floor kicking her legs about and I was doing the flat. I'd made a little tower of four coloured bricks—plastic bricks—on a rug near her head. I got on with my dusting and when I looked again I saw she'd knocked it down. I put the four bricks up again and this time watched her. First her eyes, usually moving in all directions, must have glanced in passing at this bright tower. Then the arm that side began to show real signs of intention—and her fist started clenching and—spreading—with the effort. The other arm—held here like that—(*raising one bent arm to shoulder level*)—didn't move. At all. You see the importance—she was using for the first time one arm instead of both. Must have taken—I should think

—ten minutes'—strenuous labour—to reach them with her fingers—then her hand jerked in a spasm and she pulled down the tower again. (*Reliving the episode, she puts her hands over her face to regain composure*) I can't tell you what it was like. But you can imagine, can't you? Several times the hand very nearly touched and got jerked away by spasm—and she'd try again. That was the best of it—she had a will, she had a mind of her own. Soon as Bri came home, I told him. I think he said something stupid like—you know—"That's great, put her down for piano lessons". But when he tested her—putting piles of bricks all along the circle of her reach—both arms—and even sometimes out of reach so that she had to stretch to get there—well, of course, he saw it was true. It wasn't *much* to wait for—one arm movement completed—and even that wasn't sure-fire. She'd fall asleep, the firelight would distract her, sometimes the effort would bring on a fit. But more often than not she'd manage—and a vegetable couldn't have done that. Visitors never believed it. They hadn't the patience to watch so long. And it amazed me—I remember being stunned—when I realized they thought I shouldn't deceive myself. For one thing, it wasn't deception—and anyway what else could I do? We got very absorbed in the daily games. Found her coloured balls and bells and a Kelly—those clowns that won't lie down. Then she caught some bug and was very sick—had fit after fit—the Grand Mal, not the others—what amounted to a complete relapse. When she was over it, we tried the bricks again, but she couldn't even seem to see them. That was when Bri lost interest in her. I still try, though of course I don't bother telling him. I'll tell him when something happens. It seems to me only common sense. If she did it once, she could again. I think while there's life there's hope, don't you? (*She looks towards the door up* R *again, moving a little* R) I wonder if he ever imagines what she'd be like if her brain worked. *I* do. And Bri's mother always says: "Wouldn't she be lovely if she was running about?" which makes Bri hoot with laughter. But I think of it too. Perhaps it's being a woman.

(*The* LIGHTS *go off Sheila and come up brightly over the whole set, very strong, like a continuous lightning flash.* JOE *skips on, using a rope*)

JOE (*skipping*) Mrs D, Mrs I, Mrs FFI, Mrs C, Mrs U, Mrs LTY. (*She stops skipping*) Ladies and gentlemen, there will now be an interval. Afterwards the ordinary play, with which we began the performance, will continue and we shall try to show you what happens when Sheila returns home with their mutual friends, Freddie and Pam. (*She bows, then resumes skipping, moving down* L) Charlie Chaplin went to France . . .

JOE *exits down* L, *skipping, the* LIGHTS *fade to a* BLACK-OUT, *and—*

the CURTAIN *falls*

ACT II

SCENE—*The same. Later that evening.*

When the CURTAIN *rises, the stage is in darkness.* SHEILA *opens the hall door.*

SHEILA. Just let me get the light on. (*She puts on the hall light*)

(SHEILA *enters and puts on the room lights*)

Not in here. Must be working. Miracles never cease.

(SHEILA *moves above the sofa* RC. PAM *and* FREDDIE *follow her in,* PAM *up* C, FREDDIE L *of her.* FREDDIE *is suited, school-tied, with a hearty barking humourless laugh. He is the same age as Bri, but his ample public confidence makes him seem middle-aged.* PAM *dresses well, mispronounces her words in an upper-class gabble, and her postures and manners have been taken from fashionable magazines. She uses this posture to hold her own against Freddie's heartiness. He is hearty, she is blasé*)

FREDDIE. Not here?

SHEILA. Must be working in the attic.

PAM. Or gone to bed.

FREDDIE. At ten o'clock?

SHEILA. Perhaps hiding? (*She goes to the kitchen and switches on the light*)

(FREDDIE *and* PAM *look at each other*)

(*Returning*) No. Working.

PAM (*moving a little* L) Gorgeous room.

SHELIA. Oh, Pam, no!

PAM. Absolutely gorgeous. Not the room so much, what you've done with it.

SHELIA. Cost absolutely nothing.

PAM. It's terribly P.L.U. Isn't it, darling?

SHELIA. How's that?

PAM (*crossing Freddie to the sideboard up* L) P.L.U. People Like Us. That sideboard, for instance . . .

SHELIA. Twelve-and-six.

PAM. No!

SHELIA. In a country sale.

PAM. Absolutely gorgeous. (*To Freddie*) I'm green, aren't you, darling?

FREDDIE. Yes, but how many coats of paint did you take off?

SHELIA. Three. Cream, brown and green.

PAM (*moving in to Freddie*) Lord, the plebs and their lavatory colours.

Sheila. Freddie, you don't feel I bullied you?
Freddie. What?
Shelia. Into coming back here? Sit down, Pam, do.
Freddie (*signalling for Pam to sit on the sofa*) No. Why?

(Pam *sits* R *on the sofa*)

Sheila. I feel I did. Carrying on like that. Crying. I've been going hot and cold ever since. Don't tell Bri, will you?
Freddie. What?
Sheila. How I cried.
Freddie. Not if you say so.
Sheila. Please. How d'you like your coffee?
Freddie. Half-and-half. It's nothing to be . . .
Sheila. Pam? Half-and-half?
Pam. Black, please.
Freddie (*sitting* L *on the couch*) Nothing to be ashamed of. Wish I knew how to give way more to *my* emotions. Must be years since my waterworks were turned on.
Pam. Hope so too.
Freddie. It's an enviable capacity.
Pam. Gives me the creeps, a man in tears.
Freddie (*to Sheila*) That's why you can give so much on the stage.
Sheila. Was it all right? (*She moves* L *of the couch*)
Freddie. All right? Was it all right? A bit more than *all right*, duckie.
Sheila. No, truly.
Freddie. Truly. An electric evening.
Sheila. I felt awful.
Freddie. Pam, you saw it. Was it awful?
Pam. Gorgeous, you were absolutely gorgeous.
Sheila. It's a lovely part.
Freddie. You draw on deep wells of compassion.
Sheila. You are sweet.

(Freddie *kisses Sheila's hand.* Sheila, *embarrassed, goes to the hall and calls upstairs*)

Bri! I'm making coffee, if you want some.

(Sheila *exits up* C, *closing the door.* Freddie *rises and moves up* L, *looking at the cowboy paintings as though he thought of buying one. There is a pause.* Pam *looks at Freddie*)

Freddie. Clever, these. (*He barks*) Witty. Done by Brian, you know.
Pam. That was good—about bullying you.
Freddie (*moving* C) What?
Pam. I nearly fell about when she said that.
Freddie. 'Fraid I'm not with you.

Pam. Bully you! You were so damned keen to get in here you fell out of the car!

Freddie (*moving down* L) I fell from the car because my ankle was caught in the safety-belt. (*He looks at the thalidomide child picture down* L)

(Pam *laughs and takes a cigarette from her case.* Freddie *joins in the laugh*)

That yob on the motor-bike nearly went over me.

Pam. Give me a match, will you?

Freddie (*moving to Pam*) Darling, I thought you wanted to *help* these people.

Pam. Not me, darling.

Freddie. They need help. We can afford to give it. (*He lights her cigarette*) You've been smoking like a furnace all night.

Pam. And all day. I always smoke when I'm bored.

Freddie. Don't stay if you're bored.

Pam. What do you mean?

Freddie. Well, your car's outside.

Pam. What about you?

Freddie. I'll ring for a cab when I'm ready.

Pam. I don't see a phone here, do you?

Freddie. For crying out loud, if you're bored go home.

Pam. I'm bored there too all day.

Freddie. Then interest yourself in someone else for a change. Sheila, for instance. We've done a lot for Sheila, darling, we mustn't stop now.

Pam. You, not me.

Freddie (*moving down* C *and speaking to the audience*) Well, I'm not the sort to sit around making sympathetic noises and doing sweet F.A., so naturally as soon as I heard she'd been on the stage I saw the way to help. Got her down to join the players: friendly crowd, nice atmosphere—worked like a dose of salts. So well, in fact, poor old Bri's gone slightly hatcha—thinks I'm getting my end away with Sheila.

Pam. Hardly surprising. He's left holding the baby.

Freddie. Exactly.

Pam. Literally.

Freddie. Yes, tragic. Which is why I'm here. (A) To tell him there's nothing in it. (B) Get them both to see sense about the poor kiddie. And (C) to give poor Brian back an interest in life.

(Pam *makes a face and looks at her watch*)

Pam. It's gone ten now. What sort of thing did you have in mind?

Freddie. What for?

Pam. To give him back an interest.

Freddie (*moving up* C) Ah. I thought for a starter, get him down to see his wife in the play.

PAM. Of course you're joking.
FREDDIE. No.
PAM. You told me he can't stand acting.
FREDDIE. Part of his chosen image. If he *loves* the woman—and he *claims* he does . . .
PAM. She's not even any *good* in it.
FREDDIE (*moving to Pam and pointing up* R) Will you shut up!
PAM (*after a pause, not lowering her voice*) Well, is she? He'll see in a flash you're giving her charity and he's hardly the kind of man who . . .
FREDDIE. I think I know him a shade better than you. We were at *school* together.
PAM. Same school at the same time. I wouldn't exactly call that "together".
FREDDIE (*moving downstage; to the audience*) Some truth in that. He was always in the backward classes. Spent his time in the back rows, breaking wind and so forth.
PAM. Freddie!
FREDDIE. Well, he did. And there was no need for it, he was brainy enough. Just got in with the wrong crowd. No, that sounds reactionary but you've only got to look at him. Halfway through his life and no degree, no future, not much past—coping with the arse-end of a comprehensive school and driving a fifteen-year old Popular.

(SHEILA *enters from the kitchen*)

SHEILA. Ginger cat didn't come in here?
PAM (*rising*) Haven't seen it.

(SHEILA *makes to go*)

Want helping?
SHEILA. No, thanks.

(SHEILA *exits up* R. FREDDIE *scratches his arm.* PAM *scratches her thigh and sits as before*)

FREDDIE (*moving downstage*) Not that my position's anything to boast about. I just took over the factory where Dad left off.
PAM. Oh, not quite darling. You've worked wonders.
FREDDIE. Only because I'm dead keen. But I'm not as bright as Brian, not nearly as talented. That's what's so galling to me as a Socialist. The waste! Since school, as a matter of fact, I saw nothing of him till six months ago. On a train to town. I leaned over and said: "*Dum spiro spero* mean anything to you?"
PAM. Must say it doesn't to me.
FREDDIE. Our school motto. While I live I hope.
PAM. Bit squaresville, darling.
FREDDIE (*stoutly*) I *am* a bit squaresville! Anyway—(*continuing to the audience*)—he couldn't get away and we had a good old belly-ache. Told me all about his poor kiddie and how Sheila was obsessed with her and how keen he was to get her back in the swim.

PAM. Sheila.

FREDDIE (*bewildered*) Yes.

PAM. Not the weirdie.

FREDDIE. The what?

PAM. You know.

FREDDIE. Don't call her a weirdie, darling.

PAM. I know, darling, it's absolutely horrid. But she is, though, isn't she?

FREDDIE (*moving upstage*) Try to imagine that one of ours has turned out like that.

PAM (*shocked*) Darling! They're absolutely gorgeous, how could you?

(*There is a pause, then* FREDDIE *gives up and returns to the audience, moving downstage*)

FREDDIE. I don't want to sound authoritarian or fascist but there's only one useful approach to any human problem and that's a positive one. No use saying: "This is no way to live, in every night with a hopeless cripple." No use at all. Same with problem teenagers. You don't say: "Naughty boy, go stand in the corner." You say: "Get hold of these nails and a hammer!" Then you're in business.

(BRI *opens the door up* C, *then disappears.* FREDDIE *turns.* BRI *returns with a life-size painting of a cowboy. His head is stuck through an opening in the painting, and he is holding it with his hands acting as guns.* FREDDIE *laughs.* PAM *rises*)

FREDDIE (*moving below the chaise*) Well, well!

BRI. Nice surprise, Fred. Hullo, Pam. (*He removes his head from the painting and shuts the "door" of the picture, i.e. the real head*) Nice having company. Stuck in here every night like Joe Egg.

PAM. Like who?

BRI. Joe Egg. My grandma used to say: "Sitting about like Joe Egg" when she meant she had nothing to do.

FREDDIE. We've been here ages. Didn't you hear?

BRI. I was miles away.

FREDDIE. In the attic. Sheila said you . . .

BRI. In a saloon. Painting Wild Bill Hickock. Posed for this just before sitting down to his last poker game. Look at his pose. He fancied himself, and the cards—his last hand. They shot him in the back.

FREDDIE. Very good. It really is. Very good. Witty. (*He laughs*) And this one—(*pointing to the picture on the wall*)—from the same series?

BRI (*putting the Hickock picture against the wall up* LC) Ah. That's a story picture. "Where's the bleeding bugle call?" The beleaguered fort holding out for the cavalry that never comes. Few rounds left, Sioux closing in. Inset: cavalryman smiling for the recruiting posters. (*He turns up his nose at it*) Bit preachy.

FREDDIE. Why not? If it's a message that needs . . .

BRI (*crossing down* L *to the thalidomide picture*) Rather have the pure heroic image myself. Like this one. The Thalidomide Kid. Fastest gun in the West. On the slightest impulse from his rudimentary arm-stumps, the steel hands fly to the holsters, he spins on solid rubber wheels and—pschoo! (*He blazes away*)

FREDDIE (*moving upstage*) That's a bit too sick for me.

(PAM *sits* R *on the sofa.* BRI *moves down to the audience, circling*)

Give me a good message any time.

BRI (*to the audience*) What's he doing here? (*He moves to the sofa and sits*) Hallo, Pam. I meant to do Geronimo tonight, but Joe had to be—um—attended to—and . . .

(SHEILA *enters with four coffee-cups, sugar and milk on a tray*)

—by the time I'd got her to bed, it hardly seemed worth blacking up for.

(SHEILA *moves to the coffee table with the tray.* FREDDIE *takes the tray from her and puts it on the coffee-table.* SHEILA *squats* L *of the table.* FREDDIE *sits on the wicker chair* LC)

SHEILA. You've been painting.

BRI (*defensively*) I wore my old clothes.

SHEILA. Brian, fancy saying that! I want you to paint. That's the only reason I take these parts.

BRI. How did it go—the practice?

FREDDIE. Oh, blood, sweat and tears, you know, but it's coming.

SHEILA. Did you mention Joe just then?

BRI. I said I had to attend to her.

SHEILA. You mean the usual?

BRI (*rising and moving to the sideboard*) Got some drink, haven't we?

SHEILA. Brian!

BRI (*looking in the cupboard*) What?

SHEILA (*sitting on the sofa*) You mean the usual?

BRI. Bit more than the usual.

SHEILA. What d'you mean?

BRI (*showing bottles*) Cyprus sherry or Spanish cognac. Christ!

SHEILA (*shouting*) Brian!

(BRI *stares at her*)

What d'you mean—bit more than the usual?

BRI (*shouting*) We had a row! She flounced out and slammed the door.

SHEILA. No silly jokes. She's all right?

BRI. I'd rather not talk about it. Here we are—all set for a civilized conversation and you keep on about that poor crackpot. Spanish cognac, Fred?

FREDDIE. Thanks.

BRI. Sorry, Pam?

PAM. I think I won't.

BRI (*returning to the sideboard and pouring drinks*) Sheila's parents brought it back from Torremolinos. Sure you wouldn't sooner have cider?

FREDDIE. No. Why?

BRI. I just remembered you're a Socialist. So many places you've got to boycott. Worse than entertaining an R.C.

FREDDIE. I don't go for that. Misguided. A blow against Fascism, Apartheid? Very likely! All you hurt is some poor peasant.

BRI. Three cognac coming up. (*To Freddie*) Monsieur. (*To Sheila*) Madam. (*To Pam*) Pam? Go on.

(PAM *refuses*)

Come on.

(PAM *refuses*)

Go on.

(PAM *makes a move to take the drink*)

All right, please yourself.

(BRI *moves to the chaise, sits and drinks*)

SHEILA. Brian, your shoes!

BRI. What?

SHEILA. You wore your teaching shoes and look, they're covered in paint.

BRI. Spots.

SHEILA. Just look at them! Freddie, what would Pam say if you got paint on your office shoes?

BRI. I'm sorry, honest, love.

SHEILA. You won't get it off!

BRI. I'll get it off.

SHEILA. Why don't you *think*? Go and change them, go on.

BRI. It's done now. And I'm not painting any more.

SHEILA. As though you couldn't have changed your shoes.

FREDDIE (*after a pause*) How *is* the teaching, Brian?

BRI. Oh, keep them off the street, you know. Eyes front hands on heads.

FREDDIE. You still don't like it?

BRI. It's not exactly Goodbye Mister Chips.

FREDDIE. All the same, I envy you. In many ways I often wish I'd been a teacher.

BRI. Instead of a rich and powerful industralist, yes it must be lonely.

(SHEILA *laughs to remove the sting*)

FREDDIE (*barking*) Rich? Where d'you get the idea I'm rich?

PAM. We're not *rich*.

SHEILA. Comfortable?

PAM. Comfortable, yes, not rich.

FREDDIE. Nor powerful. (*He barks*) You've been watching too much telly. No, hamstrung's nearer the mark. I'm like a last-ditch colonial running things till the natives have got enough know-how to take the reins.

BRI. That's right? (*He tut-tuts at the thought*) Don't know what the world's coming to.

FREDDIE. How are things on the home front, Bri?

BRI. Oh, much the same, you know.

FREDDIE. Stuck in like Joe Egg?

BRI. Yeah.

FREDDIE (*putting his cup and glass on the table, rising, and moving upstage*) Look—perhaps I'm rushing in where angels fear to tread . . .

PAM. You always do.

(FREDDIE *barks*)

FREDDIE. But—why don't you see all the doctors money can buy and tell them you want another baby?

(SHEILA *and* BRI *look at each other*)

To put it bluntly—ask why you're not having one.

SHEILA. Oh, we've had fertility counts. That what you mean?

FREDDIE. You've done that?

BRI. Yes. She was A minus, I was B plus. Must concentrate more.

FREDDIE. Well done. I admire your nerve. Most people wouldn't fancy knowing for sure.

SHEILA. No. 'Specially men. Our doctor had an ex-major who turned really nasty when they told him he was sub-fertile. He kept saying: "But I was in the Normandy Landings".

BRI. "I demand a recount."

FREDDIE (*barking with laughter*) Hah! Poor fellow. How absolutely terrifying. (*He sits in his chair*) How about boosters?

BRI. What?

FREDDIE. Fertility boosters.

SHEILA. No.

FREDDIE. I know a gynaecologist in London, did so well by a friend of mine his wife's applied to be sterilized.

PAM. Georgina?

FREDDIE. Lavinia. Shall I fix an appointment?

SHEILA. I don't mind.

FREDDIE. If all else fails, I'll get the adoption machinery moving. Takes some time as a rule but I can put some ginger under the right people. Get it moved to the top of the in-tray. Always back out later if you find you've hit the spot.

(SHEILA *winces*)

So—whatever happens—at least you'll have a proper working child.

Sheila (*shrugging*) Two children instead of one.

Bri. She won't like it, Mum.

Sheila. She likes to rule the roost, Dad.

Freddie (*to Sheila*) Surely, my dear, you can see you're only prepared to give up your life to little Joe because there's no-one else. Once you've got a normal healthy baby looking up at you, smiling at you—(*to Bri*)—does *she* smile?

Bri. She used to. Now and then.

Sheila. Often, often!

Freddie. A real baby will smile every time you look at her. (*To Sheila*) And she'll cry too and keep you up every night—and crawl and walk and talk and . . .

Sheila. Yes, I've seen them. What then?

Freddie. Well—then—at least you'll be in a position to decide.

Sheila. What?

Freddie. Whether to let Joe go into a residential school.

Bri. We've tried that too.

Freddie. Oh?

Sheila. Putting her away, yes.

Freddie. Don't call it that.

Sheila. What else is it?

Bri. She worried all the time, wouldn't let her stay.

Freddie. I'm on the board of a wonderful place. They're not prisons, you know, not these days. They're run by loving and devoted teachers—hideously underpaid but I'm doing what I can in that direction . . .

Sheila. I don't care how good the nurses are—she *knows*! She was ill in that place.

Bri. Change of diet.

Sheila. She was pining.

Freddie. This isn't a hospital—

(Pam *looks at her watch*)

—it's a special school.

Bri. How's the time going, Pam?

Freddie. A private house. Trees all round . . .

Pam (*to Sheila*) There was a fabulous article in Nova about it. D'you remember?

Sheila. No.

Freddie. And if she improves, she can join their activities . . .

Bri. Activities?

Freddie. Painting—wheelchair gardening—speech therapy.

Bri. Better not tell *her* that. She thinks she's very *nicely* spoken. One thing she *does* pride herself on, eh Mum?

Sheila (*to Freddie*) She wouldn't go to a special school, even if you put some ginger under them. We've seen the place she'd go to. (*To Bri*) No private house, Dad. No Palladian asylum with acres of graceful parkland.

Bri. Nor Victorian Gothic even, Mum.
Sheila. Army Surplus. Like a transit camp.
Bri. Except they're not going anywhere.
Sheila. Freddie, thanks for trying, but it's too late, honestly. I shall have to look after her till she dies.
Bri. Or until you do.
Sheila. Yes. Whichever's first.
Freddie. Is that possible?
Sheila. What?
Freddie. She could outlive you?
Sheila. We know one—a man of seventy-six, just joined the boy scouts. They wouldn't have him any longer in the cubs.

(Bri *and* Sheila *laugh*)

Freddie (*rising and moving down* c) These jokes. May I say my piece about these jokes? (*He moves up* c, *pushing his chair with his foot*) They've obviously helped you to see it through. A useful anaesthetic. But. Isn't there a point where the jokes start using *you*?
Sheila. I thought you were going to speak to Bri about . . .
Freddie. Please. This first. Isn't that the whole fallacy of the sick joke? It kills the pain but leaves the situation just as it was? Look—when we met again—how many?—six months?—ago—you used, I remember, a striking metaphor describing Sheila's state of mind. You said a cataract had closed her eye—like your mother's net curtains, screening off the world outside.
Bri. Did I say that?
Freddie. It struck me as so bloody apt.
Bri. So bloody smug.
Freddie. But it was true, don't you see? And now—in my opinion—it's all gone arse-over-tip. Sheila's cured and you've caught the cataract. Shoot me down if I'm all to cock. I'm only trying to strip it down to essentials. Thinking aloud.
Bri. I wonder—could you think more quietly?
Freddie. Am I shouting? Sorry. I tend to raise my voice when I'm helping people.
Bri. It's just that I've got a splitting headache.
Freddie (*returning to his seat*) All right. (*Addressing Bri quietly and earnestly*) When I see a young couple giving up their lives to a lost cause, it gives me the screaming habdabs. As a Socialist! The waste! I think to myself: all right, I don't care, I *am* my Brother's Keeper, I bloody well am.
Bri. Thanks, that's much quieter.

(Sheila *giggles*)

Freddie. Another joke. Another giggle.
Pam. Come on, Freddie, let's go . . .
Freddie. The whole issue's a giggle. I throw you a lifeline and you giggle. The whole country giggling its way to disaster.

Pam (*to Bri*) She broke down tonight.
Bri. What?
Freddie. Pam . . .
Sheila. You said you wouldn't . . .
Pam. In a flood of tears. (*To Freddie, starting to rise*) Come on . . .

(Freddie *rises, taking over.* Pam *sits*)

Freddie. Because she can't cope any more with your suspicions and jealousies. So I said I'd put you straight on one or two points.
Pam. Wasting your breath, darling.
Freddie. (A)—we're not going to bed together.
Bri (*to Sheila*) Scab!
Freddie. (B)—it's hardly likely because (a) she loves you,—(*moving below the couch and round it to above Pam*)—(b) I love Pam and (c) I've got three smashing kids . . . (*He puts his hand on Pam's shoulder*)
Pam. Darling, I love you too.
Freddie. And I'm hardly likely to throw all that away for a bit on the side—however gorgeous the bit may be—(*smiling at Sheila*)—and though I'm not a practising Christian, I think I know my duty.
Bri (*rising*) Yes, but Fred . . .
Freddie. And—squaresville or not—I happen to believe in duty.
Pam. Terribly sweet.

(Pam *and* Freddie *kiss*)

Bri. I hardly know how to say this now. After your masterly dismissal of jokes. But the whole idea was just another sick fantasy. I know you've never touched her, leave alone gone to bed with her.
Pam. He's a nut.
Bri. I wanted to bring back the magic to our marriage. Stir it up, an emotional aphrodisiac?
Pam (*to Freddie*) If you ever try that with me, I'll leave you.
Freddie. I may be squaresville but I'm not sick.
Sheila (*to Bri*) You're so round*about.*
Bri. You wouldn't let me near you. All day I'd been running blue movies on the back of my retina—the pair of us romping about the bed shouting with satisfaction. And what did I get when I got home? "Oh, your hands are cold!"
Pam. This is too juvenile. Let's go.
Freddie. That's what he *wants*

(Bri *moves to the sideboard for more drink*)

(*Moving down* c) But I want to *help* him. (*To the audience*) Am I wasting my time, d'you think?

(*Off-stage, children's voices sing:* "*Once in Royal David's City*")

Bri (*moving downstage above the chaise*) Listen to that.

SHEILA } (together) { Aaah!
BRI }

PAM. Aah!

(BRI *and* SHEILA *look at Pam*)

BRI. Carols at this time of night. The neighbours won't be able to hear the telly.

SHEILA. She loves the carols. Let me fetch her.

PAM (*rising*) No. We're going.

(FREDDIE *moves towards Pam.* SHEILA *rises*)

SHEILA. You've never seen her. Wouldn't you like to?

FREDDIE. I'd love to.

PAM. It's twenty past ten.

FREDDIE (*shrugging*) The *au-pair* girl will have gone to bed.

PAM. Your train in the morning.

FREDDIE. What train? Not tomorrow.

PAM. I thought it was tomorrow.

FREDDIE. No, darling. You'd like to see her, wouldn't you?

PAM. Love to. Give me a match. (PAM *sits and takes out a cigarette*)

(FREDDIE *lights Pam's cigarette.* SHEILA *moves upstage*)

BRI. Sheila, don't!

SHEILA. What?

FREDDIE (*to Pam*) You'll get lung cancer.

PAM. They're my lungs.

SHEILA. What?

BRI. I forgot to tell you what happened—while you were out.

(FREDDIE *sits by Pam on the couch. The singers go quieter*)

SHEILA. What?

BRI. Shall I tell you?

SHEILA (*sitting on the* L *edge of the couch*) Happened where?

BRI. Here. First—I fed Joe. (*To Freddie*) She was constipated. She hadn't been for weeks so I chose a nice tin of strained prunes. What my grandma used to call black-coated workers. They have to be strained still because her teeth are—a bit stumpy. After I'd got that lot down, I had a bite myself, read the paper. But she kept having little fits and whimpering so I plonked her in the nursery. I thought to myself: "Perhaps the spasm's hurting", so I tried to loosen it with exercises.

SHEILA. The constipation hurts her.

BRI (*explaining to Freddie*) The spasm's in the back between the shoulders. Sheila got this method of breaking it down from a lady wrestler she met at an Oxfam coffee party.

SHEILA (*to Freddie: with a smile*) A physiotherapist.

BRI (*taking a cushion and demonstrating with it*) You take her arms and wrap them across her chest—like so—and hold them very tight

—then push her head right forward and down till her chin's rammed in between her collar-bones. As though you were trying to make a parcel. (*He demonstrates*) I don't know whether it's any use but I faced the fact long ago that I enjoy it. Find myself smiling when she cries. At least it's a reaction. But tonight she wouldn't stop even when I let her go.

SHEILA. Those fits upset her.

BRI. So I undressed her and applied a suppository. Put a rubber sheet underneath and doubled her up like a book—pressed on her stomach to help—and at last, over half-an-hour I should think, she managed "number twos".

SHEILA. Oh, good. That was bothering her, poor love.

BRI. When it was all out, she started that gulping and lip-smacking, stretching her arms, opening and closing her blind eyes—the Grand Mal. I thought to myself, that's it, the lot! All you can do. Pain and fits. And not for the first time in ten years I thought: Is it ever worth it?

FREDDIE. Perhaps it isn't.

SHEILA. Worth what?

FREDDIE. The effort.

SHEILA. We've got no choice.

FREDDIE. Of course you have—the special schools.

(*The voices of the singers fade*)

BRI. Anyway. When the first was over, I put her down, went and stood behind her and put a cushion over her mouth and nose and pressed down and held it there while I counted a hundred. There was no struggle. It was very—peaceful.

(*The others watch Bri, motionless. There is a pause*)

SHEILA (*rising*) What . . .?

PAM. God!

(*The children off-stage sing "Noël"*)

BRI. When it was all over I took the cushion away and—I said: "Nurse, you have seen nothing. We are in this together." I looked up to see the nurse throw off her cape revealing the burly figure of Inspector Blake, Scotland Yard.

SHEILA (*relieved*) Honestly, Brian!

BRI. You almost believed me, didn't you?

FREDDIE. No almost. I *did*.

SHEILA. I should *know* by now. She *is* all right, isn't she?

BRI. Yes.

SHEILA (*starting to move upstage*) I'm going to see her.

BRI (*moving to Sheila and holding her arm*) Did you feel relieved at all, even a little bit, when you thought I'd done it?

SHEILA. Don't be silly.

Bri. Not even a teeny-weeny drop relieved to think it was all over?

Sheila. Of course not. Honestly.

(*The voices of the singers fade*)

Bri (*moving to Freddie*) How about *you*?

Freddie. What?

Bri. Were you relieved at all?

Freddie. Of course not. Horrified!

Bri. Because it would be murder?

Freddie. You can't take life, man.

Bri (*moving downstage and returning*) Her life—what is it?

Freddie. I don't care.

Bri. You've never *seen* her.

Freddie. I'd *like* to see her.

Bri. You shall in a minute.

Pam. Darling, it's half past ten.

Bri (*ignoring her*) She's not alive. What can she *do*?

Freddie. It doesn't matter.

Bri. Asphyxiation delayed ten years by drugs.

Freddie. She should be put away . . .

Bri. Everyone's always saying: "Do something", but when I make a suggestion, it's all wrong.

Freddie. If all you can suggest is murder, yes.

Bri (*moving* L *below the chaise, then round above it and above the sofa*) Living with Sheila, you get to welcome death. With life burgeoning in every cranny. (*Listing the wild-life*) Flora, fauna, gawping gold-fish—budgies—busy Lizzie—cats—cats' fleas . . .

Pam. I *knew* I'd been itching.

Bri. Fleas from Sidney and Beatrice Webb, we're not sure which. When the tom-kitten was born, Sheila wanted to call him Dick, but I drew the line there. Standing on the back steps last thing at night shouting: "Dick, Dick!" Might have got killed in the rush.

(*He goes up* L *and moves the cowboy picture a little away* L)

Freddie. There are one or two great . . .

Bri. Sheila embraces all living things. (*Hastily, to Pam*) Except Freddie. She never embraces Freddie. (*He moves in to Freddie then moves away again*)

Freddie (*rising to Bri*) I said there are one or two great moral commandments and in my view they're the only hope we've got against chaos. Love thine enemy. Thou shalt not kill.

(Bri *swats an imaginary fly from his forehead*)

D'you know how the final solution of the Jewish problem began? In the mental hospitals. It's only a step from there to Auschwitz.

Pam (*rising and moving to Freddie*) Darling—it's half past ten.

Freddie (*suddenly*) You're like a blasted speaking clock. On the third stroke—peep-peep-peep. (*He moves down* R)

(PAM *looks at* BRI, *who turns away* L)

PAM. Oh, charming.

(FREDDIE *sits in the rocking chair*, BRI *sits on the chaise*. PAM *looks at both men, who are ignoring her and each other. There is a complete separation of all three people on the stage.* PAM *comes downstage and speaks to the audience*)

It wasn't my idea coming back here in the first place. But once Freddie's set eyes on a lame dog, you might as well talk to the moon. I keep looking at that door and thinking she's going to come through it any moment with that poor weirdie. I know it's awful but it's one of my—you know—THINGS. We're none of us perfect—I can't stand anything N.P.A.—Non Physically Attractive. Old women in bathing-suits—and skin-diseases—and cripples—and Rowton House-looking men who spit and have hair growing out of their ears. No good. I just can't look at them. I know Freddie's right about Hitler and of course that's horrid. Still, I can't help sympathising with Brian, can you? I don't mean the way he described. I think it should be done by the state. And so should charity. Then we might have an end of all those hideous dolls in shop-doorways with irons on their legs . . . Freddie won't hear of it, of course. But then he loves a lame dog. Every year he buys so many tickets for the spastic raffle he wins the t.v. set and every year he gives it to an old folks' home. He used to try taking me along on his visits but I said it wasn't me at all and he gave up. One—place—we went, there were these poor freaks with—oh, you know—enormous heads and so on—and you just feel: Oh, put them out of their misery. Well, they wouldn't have survived in nature, it's only modern medicine, so modern medicine should be allowed to do away with them. A committee of doctors and do-gooders, naturally, to make sure there's no funny business, and then—if I say gas-chamber that makes it sound horrid—but I do mean put to sleep. When Freddie gets all mealy-mouthed about it, I say: "Look, darling, if one of our kids was dying and they had a cure and you knew it had been discovered in the Nazi laboratories, would you refuse to let them use it? "I certainly wouldn't. I love my own immediate family and that's all. Can't cope with any more. I want to go home and see them again. They may not be the most hard-working, well-behaved geniuses on earth but no-one in their right mind could say they were N.P.A. (*She moves* R *to Freddie, picking up her bag on the way*) Freddie, I'm going. You can get a taxi and . . .

(SHEILA *enters up* C, *carrying* JOE *in her nightdress and dressing-gown.* BRI *rises, takes Joe and puts her on the chaise.* FREDDIE *rises and moves* C)

SHEILA. Aaaah! The carols have stopped.
BRI. They've stopped, yea.

FREDDIE. This little Josephine?
SHEILA. This is Joe. Say hullo to Uncle Freddie.
FREDDIE (*shaking Joe's hand*) Hullo, Joe, what do you know?
SHEILA. Not much, I'm afraid. And Auntie Pamela.
PAM (*moving below Freddie*) She's got—really—a rather pretty face, hasn't she?
SHEILA. She's very P.L.U. when you get to know her. (*She goes to the sideboard, collects a blanket and wraps it round Joe*) Aren't you, sweetheart?
BRI. I'm lovely, she says.
SHEILA. But strangely passive tonight. You didn't forget her medicine?
BRI. You'd be strangely passive, she says, if you'd been fitting and crying and doing doots.
SHEILA. But her eyes are hardly open.
BRI (*squatting above the chaise*) Who wants to open their eyes in the middle of the night, she says. And one hour before midnight's worth two after.
SHEILA. What a shame, she missed the carol singers.
BRI. Christmas already, she says. Seems to come round quicker every year.

(SHEILA *starts singing.* BRI *joins in after the first words*)

SHEILA (*singing*) Away in a manger, no crib for a bed,
The little Lord Jesus laid down his sweet head.
The stars in the bright sky looked down where he lay,
The little Lord Jesus asleep in the hay.
The cattle are lowing . . .

Hello.
FREDDIE. What is it?
SHEILA. A fit. I thought she was too far gone for that.
FREDDIE. Nothing we can do?
BRI (*to Joe*) You do that one day the wind will change and you'll stay like it.
SHEILA. D'you think she needs the doctor?
BRI. She should be in bed. I'll take her up.
SHEILA. What good's that? She's nearly unconscious.
BRI. What good's she doing down here?

(*The front-door bell rings*)

(*rising and moving up* C) That'll be the carol singers. I'll go. I'll say we're Muslims.

(PAM *sits*)

SHEILA. Give them a shilling from Joe.
BRI. A shilling.
SHEILA. I love the old customs, she says.

Freddie (*giving Brian a coin*) Here—from Joe.

(Bri *takes the coin awkwardly, waves it at Pam, and exits*)

I'd no idea she was so . . .

Pam (*rising*) We must be going.

Freddie. I'd no idea she was so—torpid. One thinks of a mongol or an athetoid or monoplegic. But—well—she really is *so* helpless.

(*He moves below the sofa*)

Sheila. She's worse than usual, aren't you, blossom?

(Bri *enters up* c)

Bri (*making frantic gestures and moving* r *towards the kitchen*) Action stations. It's my mother.

(Grace *follows Bri in. She is sixty-five, suburban, fastidious. She wears a light-coloured suit with frilled decorations: gloves and shoes match handbag. She is very short-sighted but refuses to wear spectacles. As well as her bag, she brings in a hold-all full of shopping. Her manner is generally bright, but gives way to spells of gloom when she tends to sigh a lot. In her presence, Bri is more boyish and struggles to escape her maternal allure*)

Sheila (*rising*) Hullo. How nice to see you!

Grace. I'm not stopping, Sheila—oh, you didn't say you had company.

Bri. Mr and Mrs Underwood, my mother.

Pam. We were just going.

Freddie. How d'you do?

Grace (*putting her handbag on the chaise, then crossing down* l *and putting her shopping bag on the chair down* l) No, I'm not stopping. Only I've been in town and thought I'd drop in Josephine's new cardie.

(Sheila, Pam, Bri *and* Freddie *sit down, facing upstage.* Bri *sits on the back of the sofa,* Pam *and* Freddie *on the sofa,* Sheila *on the chaise*)

(*Moving down* c *and speaking to the audience*) No, well, I wouldn't have dropped in, not in the ordinary way, especially when they had company, only on Tuesday Mrs Parry and I make a habit of meeting for the pictures if there's anything nice. Well, after you've been round with a duster, there's nothing much to fill in the afternoons and no-one wants to sit about like a mutt and don't laugh, will you, but they reduce the prices for old-age pensioners. I don't know whether anyone sees themself as an old-age pensioner—I know I don't but when you're trying to manage on so little, a few shillings is a consideration. Not that my husband ever thought I'd be hard up—he paid enough for his private pension and his insurance in case something happened to him first—but there, they *say* it's the middle classes that have suffered the most, don't they, from inflation? Anyway, last week Mrs Parry rang and says she couldn't see me Tuesday

—that was on the Thursday—or was it Friday?—as she had to stay in for a vacuum. I said "But surely to goodness a vacuum can come in the morning or any other afternoon, it doesn't have to be the very day we go out." She said: "My dear, nowadays if you're told to expect a vacuum Tuesday there's very little you can say to stop it." So I said: "Well, all right, I'll do some last-minute Christmas shopping in the afternoon and meet you in the Odeon café—what—about half-past four?—and we can see Julie Andrews in the evening." Then—over the week-end I finished the cardigan I'd been knitting Josephine. Well—knitting passes the time and if you don't have some diversion, you'd sit around like a blooming nun. No company, no-one to talk to or have a cup of tea with. (*She sighs, wipes her nose and dabs the corners of her mouth*) I don't encourage the neighbours. One thing can so easily lead to another with neighbours, you find them taking advantage. So it *is* very lonely, hour after hour, stuck like Joe Egg with no one to talk to. (*She goes* L, *takes the cardigan from the shopping-bag and returns* C) Why I do so many cardigans, the poor mite dribbles. Not in the way a baby dribbles even, worse than that. It's not nice to talk about, I know, but she can't seem to regulate the flow. Her garments, after a few hours on, they're stiff with saliva. (*She dabs the corners of her mouth*) Which means a lot of washing for her mother and I've said to Sheila often enough: "She should wear a plastic bib, it would be such a saving on wool", but of course you can't say a lot, can you, that's being an interfering mother-in-law. I do believe if I said: "Sheila, whatever you do, don't dress her in plastic bibs", that poor mite would be stuck in a plastic bib morning, noon and night like a blooming nun. (*She moves upstage*)

(BRI *rises and stands above the couch.* SHEILA *rises*)

(*Speaking to the others*) And when we came out of the Odeon, I thought I'll go so far on Mrs Parry's bus and drop in with my granddaughter's cardigan and p'raps if Brian's not too busy he could run me home.

BRI. Yes, right.

GRACE. So I'm not stopping. (*She sits on the chaise by Joe*) And how's Nana's favourite girl tonight? Look what Nana's brought her. I'm fast asleep, she says.

SHEILA. She's poorly, very poorly.

GRACE. Having forty winks, she says.

BRI. She's all right.

GRACE. An hour before midnight's worth two after.

BRI. That's what they say.

GRACE. Let's see how it fits, shall we? (*She holds the cardigan against Joe*) Wouldn't she be lovely if she was running about?

FREDDIE. A beautiful child.

GRACE. First time you've seen her?

SHEILA. Why I brought her down.

GRACE. D'you think the sleeves are short, Sheila?

SHEILA (*moving* R *and sitting on the sofa*) Her arms are so bent.

GRACE. You must allow for that, yes. I should say a half-inch longer.

SHEILA. Would you bother?

GRACE. No bother. Got to do what little we can, haven't we?

FREDDIE. Yes, exactly.

GRACE (*rising and moving* C) You should have seen the shops this afternoon. I said to the lady in Scotch Wool and Hosiery: "You'll be glad when Christmas is over?"

BRI. What did she say?

GRACE. "I certainly will," she said.

(BRI *shakes his head slowly in amazement*)

But apart from the rush, I said to Mrs Parry, it does look nice—the decorations and toys and turkeys and toilet sets.

BRI. See Jesus?

GRACE. Pardon?

BRI. Did you see Jesus?

GRACE (*moving back to Joe without looking at Bri; cautiously*) Well, if I did I didn't notice.

BRI. On the electricity building.

GRACE (*moving* C; *tut-tutting*) They'll drag religion into anything, won't they? (*She pauses, looking at the cardigan*) Colour's nice, isn't it? I think that sort of thing spoils Christmas.

BRI. Jesus?

GRACE (*making herself clear*) I think it's a time for the children. Brian, d'you remember the very first year I took you to see Father Christmas?

BRI. Um . . .

GRACE. I shall never forget it. He took one look at him and said: "Mummy, I don't like that funny man".

(FREDDIE *laughs politely*. BRI *might not have heard*)

But you loved the toy department. You used to say: "Oh, mummy, I want it all, can I have it, mummy, all to myself?" (*She sits in the wicker chair*)

(SHEILA *laughs*)

BRI (*moving down* R *and sitting in the rocking chair*) We took Joe to Father Christmas. He stank of meths and he was handing out foam-rubber pandas and patting all the little girls on their knees.

FREDDIE (*rising and moving down* L) Why do you say these things?

BRI. It's true!

FREDDIE. It is *not* true. They're vetted.

BRI. We've got one.

FREDDIE. What?

BRI. It sits in any position.

FREDDIE. Not the pandas. The—other . . .

BRI. That was true. Soon as Joe sat on his lap, she had a fit. That stopped him.

GRACE (*to Sheila; scratching herself*) D'you know, I believe I've acquired a little visitor? Not what you expect from the Odeon.

BRI. You got it here. Off our cat. We're infested with them.

GRACE (*rising*) Are you really, Sheila? Fleas is something I don't believe we've ever had. Can you remember, Brian?

BRI. An occasional wood-louse.

GRACE (*moving about nervously*) Not the same as fleas.

SHEILA. It's Beatrice Webb. We keep her outside now.

GRACE. I should. I know you're very fond of animals, Sheila, but surely it's an interest you must keep in proportion.

SHEILA. It's the first time we've ever had them.

GRACE. There's a first time for everything, isn't there? (*Going to Joe*) Isn't there, loveliest girl in all the wide wide world?

SHEILA (*rising and moving to the chaise*) Look! Another fit.

GRACE (*moving backwards*) Bless her heart! (*She moves up* L *of the couch*)

SHEILA (*examining Joe*) She's worse. Look at this.

BRI. She's sleeping it off. (*To Grace*) You see, Mum, they left off her medicine at the centre today.

SHEILA (*moving* R *above the sofa*) How can you say that?

BRI. What?

SHEILA. Sleeping it off.

GRACE. I should have it destroyed.

SHEILA. Another dose of medicine.

(SHEILA *exits to the kitchen*)

GRACE. If it was me.

BRI (*rising the crossing to the chaise*) Eh, you what, Mum?

GRACE. I should have whatever-you-call-her put to sleep.

BRI (*pointing at Grace*) Aah.

FREDDIE. The cat.

BRI. Oh.

GRACE. Fleas bring disease.

(BRI *sits by Joe and examines her intently*)

PAM. In my daughter's primary school, they had a plague of bugs brought in by some poor council-house kiddies.

FREDDIE (*moving below the chaise to* C) Darling, how do you know it was them?

PAM. What?

FREDDIE. The council-house kiddies.

PAM. It wasn't the kiddies' fault.

GRACE. I blame the parents.

PAM. Emma got the most hideous rash.

GRACE. Some children are more susceptible, more sensitive. Brian always had a delicate skin.

Bri. Oh, Mum!

Grace. Look at his impetigo.

(Sheila *enters* R *with an empty bottle and moves to* Bri *above the chaise*)

Sheila. What's this? The bottle's empty.

Bri. Oh, yeah! She spilt it. Joe. Knocked it over. (*After a pause*) Having a fit. I had to save her first.

Sheila. But it's like treacle. How did it get poured out?

Bri. Well, it did.

Sheila. It's been washed clean.

Bri. I saved enough to give her a dose, then washed it out.

(*There is a pause.* Sheila *puts the bottle on the sideboard*)

Sheila. You must get some more.

Bri. She's had enough sedation for one night.

(*They all look at him*)

I'm turned on, she says.

Sheila. She's having fits.

Bri. Not bad ones.

Sheila. They weaken her. She needs the anti-convulsant.

Bri. All very well, but what time is it? Pam?

Pam. Twenty to eleven.

Bri. There you are!

Grace. Boots is open. On the Centre.

Freddie. Shall I go?

Bri (*rising*) No, I'll go. (*He moves up* c)

(Sheila *picks up the prescription from the sideboard and gives it to Bri*)

Sheila. Here's the prescription.

Grace. I should wrap up warm, Bri. Put a scarf on.

(Bri *starts to go*)

Sheila. Get a move on.

(Bri *exits up* c)

Grace (*moving down and sitting next to Pam*) He's always been a martyr to colds. I've known him come in crying with his poor little fingers all yellow, and all the other boys still out running about, and I've had to rub them and get him a warm drink and sit him by the fire till he was over it . . .

(Sheila *sits on the chaise and holds Joe's hand*)

Sheila. What's funny daddy been up to, eh, my rose?

(*There is a pause.* Freddie's *attention is drawn to Sheila's remark*)

Freddie (*squatting above the chaise*) You think he's up to something?

Sheila. That medicine's thick. You couldn't spill it all. The bottle was full, I don't know. He *told* us he'd killed her.

Freddie. That wasn't true, so we needn't . . .

Grace. Told you what?
Sheila. He'd killed her. Yes.
Grace. Oh, no.
Freddie (*rising*) It was an adolescent joke.
Grace. His jokes, I never listen.
Freddie. Showing off to get attention.
Grace. It is, it's showing off.
Sheila. Like a baby. By saying that he could take my attention off poor Joe and get it on himself again. And when that palled, he'd make up another—with himself as the killer or the corpse or—anything—as long as it's the most important part.
Grace. I don't think Brian would say a thing like that without provocation.
Freddie (*moving to Grace*) No. Well the other joke we've had this evening was that Sheila and I are having a love affair. And for that, I assure you, we neither of us gave him the slightest provocation.
Grace. Well, perhaps not *you*. I couldn't say.
Sheila. Hullo?
Grace. But I shouldn't wonder if Brian thought there was something—going on . . .
Freddie. Why?
Grace. Perhaps—knowing what he did—he was apt to be over-suspicious.

(Sheila *rises and moves* L *of the sofa.* Freddie *moves a little upstage*)

Sheila. Knowing what he . . .
Grace. Probably expect it. (*To Pam*) I mean always. Half expected it.
Sheila. What d'you mean?
Grace. No. Nothing.
Sheila. Come on.
Freddie (*moving above the sofa*) Frankly, I resent the . . .
Grace. I didn't mean to say that, no . . .
Sheila. Why should he have expected it?
Grace. Don't you know?
Sheila. No.
Grace. I think you *do*, Sheila. Brian knew all about your past life even before he married you.
Sheila. Of course he did. *I* told him.
Grace. Yes.
Sheila. How do *you* know?
Grace. He told me.
Freddie (*moving* R *of the sofa*) Lord above!
Sheila. I'd love to have heard what you said when he told you.
Pam. This is horrid.
Freddie (*to Pam*) Have you heard the car start?
Grace. I'll tell you.
Pam (*to Freddie*) I haven't, no.

Freddie (*moving up* c) I'll go and see.
Grace. I said: "You must make up your own mind, Brian.
Freddie (*to Sheila*) Going to help Brian.

(Freddie *exits up* c)

Sheila. Bet you had a shock when he did.
Grace. Meaning what exactly?
Sheila. Meaning you always made up his mind for him.
Grace (*to Pam*) *This* is nice.
Sheila. You spoilt him.
Grace. I must say!
Sheila. Wrecked him.
Grace. Thank you.

(*There is a silence. Both women are momentarily spent*)

Sheila. Where's Freddie?
Pam. He's gone to help with the car. It hadn't started.
Sheila. Not started . . . (*She moves up* c)

(Bri *and* Freddie *enter*)

Bri (*moving* l *above the chaise*) Can't get it started.
Freddie (*moving* r *above the sofa*) Have you tried, I wonder? You were sitting in it doing nothing when I saw you.
Pam (*rising*) Let me go. In my car.
Sheila (*to Pam*) Would you?
Pam (*moving upstage*) I should have gone before. (*Aside*) Anything to get away.
Bri. Shall I come—show you a short cut?
Pam. No need.

(Pam *moves up* c. Sheila *moves below* r *of the sofa*)

Freddie. Got the chitty?
Pam. What?
Freddie (*to Bri*) Give her the prescription.

(Bri *gives a prescription to Pam*)

Sheila. It's yellow, looks like custard.
Pam. This isn't it. (*She returns to to Bri*)

(Bri *finds the right prescription, starts to give it to Pam, but drops it,* Freddie *picks it up.* Pam *takes it and exits*)

Bri (*moving to the sofa and sitting* r *of Grace*) Twenty-five quid that car cost me and after only three years look at it!

(Sheila *moves* c)

Grace. You were never very clever with your hands. You took after your father there. (*To Freddie*) Poor old thing used to spend hours on end behind the radiogram and in the end we'd have to call the proper man.
Sheila (*to Bri; suddenly and vehemently*) Great baby! Great coddled baby!

Freddie. Now, Sheila . . .

Sheila (*to Freddie*) The only way he knows to get what he wants is screaming and stamping his feet, but that's a bit grotesque at his age so he straightaway says Poor Me but nobody listens so he makes some jokes and everybody laughs, which is better than nothing, so he makes more and more jokes and when everyone else has gone I get the "poor me", I have to swallow that. (*She turns on Grace*) Because you *spoilt* him.

Freddie. Sheila . . .

Grace. I kept the house free of fleas, I admit that. I spring-cleaned every year instead of once in five. Certainly when he was a tiny mite I used to press his ears back for fear they'd protrude. I boiled a kettle in his room for croup. Made a mustard bath for the cold and kept out the wind. I believe in an insulated house. (*To Bri*) It's still insulated, Brian, it's still home. You're welcome, I've told you that. Specially since I was left alone. Not so much a home these days as a blooming nunnery. I'm stuck up there day after day like a blooming nun.

Sheila (*to Freddie*) There you are. "Poor me"!

Freddie. Sssh!

Grace. What did you say?

Sheila. Your self-pity. Just like him. Poor me!

Grace. Wait till *you're* alone.

Sheila. Why don't you move in with your friend?

Grace. Mrs Parry?

Sheila. Yes. Why not? There you are, both in your perfectly insulated houses each with your own t.v. and stove and lawn-mower and empty garage, each complaining continually about being a blooming nun. What's stopping you?

Grace. You want your privacy.

Sheila. Do you? I don't. I hate it.

Grace. Wouldn't do if we were all alike.

Sheila (*to Freddie; suddenly*) You see their selfishness! We're talking them again, d'you notice? Here's Joe—(*crossing to the chaise*)—I think she's seriously ill—and—what are we doing? (*Noticing Joe again, she stops, goes down by her, looks at her closely*)

Grace. Has the poor mite ever been anything *but* seriously ill?

Sheila. We must call the doctor. She's white as chalk but her lips are blue. Straining the heart, you see.

Bri (*rising and moving to the chaise*) I'll take her back to bed, let her sleep it off.

Sheila. Her chest is hardly moving.

Bri. A touch of flatulence, she says.

Sheila (*moving away a little*) No.

Bri. Heartburn.

(Sheila *stares at Bri.* Bri *goes to pick up Joe*)

Sheila. Leave her!

(BRI *leaves Joe*)

GRACE. She ought to be in hospital.

SHEILA. I'll go if nobody else will.

GRACE. Ought to have gone in years ago.

SHEILA (*to Freddie*) But don't let Brian touch her.

GRACE. Then the marriage would have had a chance.

(SHEILA *refuses to rise to this remark and moves to the door up* C)

You can't expect a man to take second place to a child like that.

(SHEILA *exits and starts to go upstairs*)

It's not *his* fault she's spastic.

(SHEILA *enters*)

SHEILA. What was that? Not *his* fault? Whose then?

GRACE. No-one's.

SHEILA. Come on, come on.

(BRI *sits on the chaise and feels Joe's pulse*)

GRACE. I didn't mean that. Not your fault either. You can't help the family you were born into. When it's congenital it's not your fault, no . . .

SHEILA (*to Freddie*) What's she talking about?

GRACE. Fits I'm talking about.

(*There is a pause*)

SHEILA. What?

GRACE. Your uncle's fits.

SHEILA. Uncle's fits—which uncle?

GRACE. Which uncle was it, Brian?

SHEILA (*turning to Bri*) You told her my uncle had fits?

BRI. Oh, Mum!

GRACE. You did.

BRI (*to Sheila*) Your cousin Geoff.

SHEILA. Infant convulsions. What baby doesn't have infant convulsions?

GRACE. Well, none of the babies in *our* family, for a start!

SHEILA. I take that for granted, dear. (*To Bri*) What made you mention cousin Geoff to her like that? You know she'd . . .

BRI (*nodding, pacifying*) She'd just been telling *me* about the epilepsy in our family.

GRACE. I beg your pardon?

BRI (*rising and moving* C) And I felt I had to console her by mentioning someone on your side. You pick your time to throw it back, don't you?

GRACE. Epilepsy in our family? Where d'you get that?

BRI. From you! Uncle Neville.

GRACE. Uncle Neville! Oh! (*She laughs*)

BRI. Yes, Uncle Neville.

GRACE. Uncle Neville. He was never family. He just happened to marry Auntie May, that's all.

Bri. So our family's only epileptic by marriage!

Grace (*agreeing readily*) Of course! But I will say this for May. She didn't have children. Mrs Parry said to me: "I think if you know there'a taint in the family you should refrain from children."

Sheila. She'd welcome any excuse—that walking sheath! (*She moves up* c)

Grace. Don't use language to me. Honestly, Brian, you stand about like a mutt while she picks on your mother in company.

Bri. Not you, Mum—Mrs Parry.

Grace. My best friend.

Bri (*getting onto the wicker chair*) You don't expect me to defend Mrs Parry. (*As a Mad Doctor*) Nurse, nurse, we've done it, I tell you! With this we can make whole continents barren. The deterrent they've all been working for—Mrs Parry! (*He gives a Mad Laugh, and gets off the chair*)

(*There is a pause*)

Grace. I thought you were serious for a moment.

Bri. Come on. I'll run you home.

Grace (*startled*) What? Back to the nunnery.

Bri. That's right, yes.

(Grace *becomes tearful now that she knows which side Bri is on*)

Grace (*rising*) Thank you. That's gratitude.

Freddie (*moving to Bri*) I thought you said you couldn't start the car.

Bri. No, but if I crank it . . .

Freddie. You mean you didn't crank it before . . .

(Freddie *and* Sheila *look at each other*)

Grace. I had a tartan grip. Where's my tartan grip?

Bri. Over there, on the chair.

(Grace *moves* l *to pick up the cardigan from the chaise and her grip from the chair down* l)

Sheila. What about Joe? You leaving Freddie alone with her?

Bri (*moving upstage a little*) Why? You going somewhere?

Sheila. To phone the doctor.

Bri. I'll do that when I get back. If you really want to bother him.

Sheila. No, we'll do it now.

Bri. I'll only *be* twenty minutes.

Sheila. Half-an-hour, if we're *lucky*. She'll make tea.

(Grace *moves* c, *above the chaise, to below Bri*)

Bri. I shan't stop for tea.

Grace. I've got some Garibaldis, I know you . . .

Bri. Look, Mum, I can ring from your place, all right?

Grace (*moving to the sofa*) When have I ever said no to you?

(*She sits on the sofa*)

Bri (*to Sheila*) All right?

Sheila. No. We'll do it now.

Freddie. *I'll* phone the doctor.

Bri. Eh?

Freddie. While you're taking your mother home. From a local phone box.

Sheila. Would you, Freddie?

Freddie. Surely.

Bri. You interfering bastard!

Freddie. I'm trying to help you.

Bri (*moving down to Freddie*) Help? You're a pain in the arse.

Sheila (*moving above the sofa*) Has anyone got a sixpence?

(Freddie *searches in his pockets for money as they talk*)

Grace. I might have one in my bag. (*She searches also*)

Freddie (*pointing to Joe*) What you're suggesting is no way out.

Bri. There's no other possible way.

Freddie. Once start that—we'll have anarchy.

Bri. That'd be something.

Freddie. Suppose euthanasia was legalized and your daughter let die.

Bri. Yep, yep.

Freddie. Then twenty years from now a cure is found.

Grace. I could have sworn I had a sixpence.

Sheila (*moving to Freddie*) How about you, Freddie?

Bri. You mean her brain starts working?

Freddie. Just imagine that. (*To Sheila*) What?

Sheila. A sixpence.

Bri. A six-week old brain in a thirty-year old body.

Freddie (*searching in his pockets*) Nothing but half-crowns and pennies.

Sheila. My bag's upstairs.

(Sheila *exits up* c)

Grace. Aah!

(Sheila *enters*)

Freddie (*to Bri*) What?

Bri. A six-week old brain in a thirty-year old body.

Freddie. No, some kind of grafting.

Bri. Grafting?

Sheila (*to Grace*) Any luck?

Freddie. They graft kidneys. Why not brains?

Grace (*taking out a milk check from her bag*) What's this?

Sheila. A milk check. Give me a shilling.

Bri. You mean a grafted adult brain?

Sheila (*to Grace*) That's a halfpenny.

Grace (*searching*) This light's so dim.

Freddie. I don't know—yes.

BRI. I see.

GRACE (*scratching, and handing her bag to Sheila*) These nasty creatures itching. You look.

BRI. Say the brain of a woman who died at thirty?

FREDDIE. Maybe.

BRI. Whose soul do you think she'd have?

SHEILA. No, nothing here. (*She returns the bag to Grace*)

BRI. I think that question should go to our resident t.v. mini-bishop. Your Grace, would you like to say a few words?

FREDDIE. You must have order. Thou shalt not kill.

GRACE (*to Sheila*) I could have sworn there was some small silver.

BRI (*to Freddie*) Except when it shall come to pass that thy trade routes shall be in jeopardy.

SHEILA (*moving to Bri*) Bri, have you got a sixpence?

BRI (*searching, but pressing his argument*) Then shalt thou slay as many as possible of the enemies of I.C.I. and General Motors. (*He gives Sheila a sixpence*)

SHEILA (*giving Freddie the sixpence*) Here Freddie . . .

BRI. Let's have that, Fred . . .

(BRI *tries to grab the coin back. They struggle*)

FREDDIE (*throwing the sixpence back to Bri*) What are we doing? I'll dial emergency. The hospital.

SHEILA. Yes, of course! Say it's urgent. We need an ambulance.

(FREDDIE *and* SHEILA *exit up* C)

GRACE. Put a coat on, though. It's bitter.

(*But* FREDDIE *and* SHEILA *have gone.* BRI *moves up to the door after them. When* GRACE *speaks, he returns slowly to the chaise*)

And wrap yourself up properly too, Brian, if you're running me home. (*She takes from her handbag cosmetic articles and spends the next few minutes doing her face, hardly aware of what is happening behind her*) Going out of the warm on a night like this is the best way if you want to catch cold. We came out of the Odeon and it was cutting down Union Street like a knife.

(BRI *hardly listening, goes to Joe and listens for her heart, feels her pulse*)

I said to Mrs Parry: "Oh, my Lord, what a night!" She said they said we were in for something of the sort possibly lasting into February. I said: "It's a shame for the old people" and she said: "Grace, I hate to remind you, but we're the old people now". I said: "Well, if I've got to stand about waiting for buses in this, I shall catch my death."

(BRI *looks up.* GRACE *goes on making up.* BRI *looks at Joe, then towards the front door. As* GRACE *speaks,* BRI *picks Joe up, goes upstage, looks round, then decides to take her to the kitchen*)

I said: "I may be old but I'm not quite ready to go yet." So if you're running me, I should put on something warm because it's not so much the cold as the contrast.

(BRI *exits to the kitchen, slamming the door behind him.* GRACE *looks round, sees that he has gone, and continues to the audience*)

Talking to myself. No, but it's an old car with no heater and draughts from all directions and he's always been susceptible to cold.

(SHEILA *enters from the front-door and comes into the room*)

Well, if it's in your nature, I say it's nothing to be ashamed of, do you?

SHEILA. Where's Joe?

GRACE. Pardon?

SHEILA. Joe's gone.

GRACE. How can she have gone? (*She looks, and sees that Joe has*)

SHEILA. He's taken her. Where?

(*During the following,* BRI *carries* JOE *across from up* R *behind Sheila, from the back door of the house to the front door*)

GRACE. He didn't say.

SHEILA (*angrily*) Didn't you see him go?

GRACE. One minute I was talking to him, next I was talking to myself.

(SHEILA *turns, goes to the bottom of the stairs and calls*)

SHEILA. Bri!

(SHEILA *exits and runs upstairs*)

GRACE. I expect he's put her to bed, poor mite. She shouldn't be sitting up here all hours, I thought that when I came in. (*To the audience*) Brian's Dad used to say—when he was getting on: "Grace, I've had my life, if only I could give her what's left to me, I would." I believe he meant it too. Though, of course, as it turned out, there wasn't much left because he died the following year.

(BRI *enters from the front door*)

BRI. You ready, Mum?

GRACE. What?

BRI. Ready to go, are you?

GRACE. I'm getting ready.

BRI. Put your coat on then.

GRACE. Aren't you going to put one on?

BRI. No time. I'll try and get the engine started.

GRACE. You know what that engine's like. Get that started first.

SHEILA (*off*) Bri!

GRACE (*suddenly remembering*) What have you done with Josephine?

(BRI *runs off to the kitchen, closing the door,* SHEILA *enters up* C *from upstairs*)

SHEILA. He's not up there. Not anywhere. He must have gone outside.

GRACE. He's just been here.
SHEILA. With Joe?
GRACE. No.
SHEILA. Where's he gone?
GRACE. Out there.
SHEILA. The garden . . .?

(SHEILA *exits up* R, *leaving the door open*)

GRACE (*running after Sheila*) Oh, mind the cats. (*She shuts the kitchen door and scratches herself*)

(BRI *enters up* C *with Grace's overcoat*)

BRI. Ready, Mum?
GRACE. What on earth's the rush? Have you got the car running?
BRI. Let's get inside first. I can push it if it won't go.
GRACE. Mind you don't strain yourself.
BRI. Put your coat on.
GRACE. Sheila's just gone off to the garden after you.
BRI. Get a move on. (*He puts Grace's coat on her*)
GRACE. What have you done with the baby?
BRI. Me? Nothing. Hasn't Sheila got her?
GRACE. Sheila's *looking* for her.

(BRI *has by now got Grace's coat on her*)

I've got to talk to Sheila about the cardigan.
BRI. Not now, Mum. (*He collects her stuff and is about to go*) Come on! Let's go!
GRACE. Aren't you waiting for your friend to come?
SHEILA (*off*) Bri!
GRACE. Here's Sheila now.

(BRI *runs off up* C *with Grace's carrier.* SHEILA *enters up* R)

SHEILA. No sign of them. It's snowing now.
GRACE. Snowing? My Lord! Brian, I should put something on . . . (*She looks round and sees that Brian has gone*)
SHEILA. Was he here?
GRACE. Where's he gone now?
SHEILA. With Joe?
GRACE. Must have gone to the car.
SHEILA. Did he have Joe with him?
GRACE. No. He hadn't seen her. He was rushing me off my feet, but I said "I must ask Sheila whether she wants anything else—

(SHEILA *goes to the hall to look for Bri*)

done to Josephine's cardigan—apart from the sleeves . . ."

(*There is an explosion in the kitchen—not very loud, but loud enough to stop* GRACE *speaking and cause* SHEILA *to come back into the room. It is followed by the sounds of crockery or glass falling*)

My Lord . . .

Sheila. There he is!

Grace. Sounded more like the gas. D'you leave the gas on?

(Sheila *exits to the kitchen.* Grace *follows*)

Mind you don't let the cats in.

Sheila (*off*) All this glass and stick!

Grace. What is it?

(Grace *exits after Sheila, closing the door.* Freddie *and* Pam *enter up* c, Pam *carrying a bottle of yellow medicine*)

Freddie. Must be upstairs.

Pam. But why the front door open?

(Sheila *enters from the kitchen*)

Freddie. Ah! They're sending an ambulance.

Pam. The front door's open.

(Grace *enters from the kitchen*)

Freddie. I met Pam coming in.

Grace. What a mess!

Freddie. What?

Grace. Glass and sticky stuff.

Sheila. The ginger-beer plant exploded.

Grace. I thought it sounded more like the gas.

Sheila. Brian must have put a screwtop on. I've told him to use a cork. It gives when the pressure builds up.

Grace. Nuisance—anything like that with a life of its own.

Freddie. Where *is* Brian?

Sheila. He's gone mad. He's running about outside. With Joe.

Freddie. Outside?

Pam. D'you know it's snowing again?

Freddie. We didn't see him.

Pam. The door was open.

Sheila. Snowing . . .

(Sheila *moves up* c, *but* Bri *enters, carrying* Joe)

Bri (*putting Joe on the chaise*) I think it's all over.

Freddie (*moving towards Bri*) What's all over?

Bri. You look at her.

(Sheila *sits beside Joe, warming her and wrapping her about with the blanket*)

Sheila. My poor blossom . . .

Freddie (*quietly and authoritatively*) What happened?

Bri. I took her outside.

Freddie. And did what?

Bri. Nothing. (*He moves above the* l *end of the chaise*) Left her lying on the back seat of the car.

Freddie. What for?

Sheila (*to Joe*) Little worm—poor little worm . . .

BRI. Something Mum said suggested it . . .

GRACE. Me? I never suggested taking . . .

BRI. No.

GRACE. On a night like this?

BRI. But you said . . .

GRACE. Is it likely?

BRI. You said it was bitter cold. I was going to leave her in the garden but I couldn't—

SHEILA. Can anyone do the kiss of life?

FREDDIE. I can't.

BRI.—so in the end I put her in the car. I don't know what I wanted—just to stop them saving her again. When you went to phone . . .

FREDDIE (*to Sheila, crossing below the chaise to* L *of it*) Can you feel a pulse?

(BRI *moves upstage to above the sofa*)

SHEILA. No. I can't. Oh, my poor dove. She's freezing.

FREDDIE. The shock might have done it.

GRACE. Oh, my Lord. Brian, whatever made you do a thing like that?

FREDDIE. Has anyone got a looking-glass?

(GRACE *points to her handbag on the sofa.* BRIAN *moves further* R *and stands above the rocking chair*)

SHEILA. Come along, my bird, my little dove . . .

(FREDDIE *goes and searches in Grace's bag*)

GRACE. Oh, Brian, you shouldn't, not however bad she was, poor little mite, you shouldn't deliberately do that.

FREDDIE. Here's a glass. (*He goes to Sheila with a mirror, wiping it*)

SHEILA (*holding the mirror by Joe's mouth*) Sweetheart, come on, sweetheart, try for Mummy—come on, dearest love, gonna be all right now . . .

(BRI *sits in the rocking chair*)

GRACE. Perhaps the glass isn't cold enough. To get the condensation. A piece of fluff . . .

PAM. What?

GRACE. A feather will show the slightest draught. (*She searches in the sofa cushions for a feather*)

PAM. This is ghastly.

GRACE. Is this a feather?

FREDDIE. Yes.

GRACE (*giving the feather to Sheila*) There. Close to her mouth. This is how we knew poor Dad had gone.

(*The front-door bell rings*)

FREDDIE. Here they are. Don't say anything, anyone. I'll answer all the questions. You concentrate on the child. No need for unnecessary suffering. All right?

(Freddie *picks up* Joe *and exits up* c)

Sheila (*following*) Come along, now.

(Sheila *exits up* c)

Grace (*to* Pam) Wouldn't she have been lovely if she'd been running about?

(Grace *and* Pam *exit up* c)

Bri (*to the audience*) Sheila and I went with Joe in the ambulance. Mum stayed in Pam's car waiting for news. (*He rises and moves down* c) It was all-stations go in the hospital—voluntary women rushing everywhere with soup and Bibles. St Bernards standing by. (*He mimes holding a hand-mike and assumes an awe-stricken voice*) If there *is* anything heartening about such a disaster, I think it's the wonderful way this great operation of mercy has moved into action. And of course the uniquely British optimism that suddenly in moments of crisis seems to suffuse the whole nauseating atmosphere. I remember—when they first came in—the husband was jibbering and shaking like some spineless dago but nobody quite knew what to do. Then one of the impressive Lesbian nurses pointed to the African orderlies and said quietly: "Pull yourself together, man, set an example." (*He drops the parody*) Anyway, the sawbones got to work with the oil-can and: "I think there's a chance, nurse—all our work may not be wasted." And the upshot was—Mum's feather finally fluttered. Sheila could hardly stand, what with anxiety and relief, so they gave her a bed for the night. Joe was staying in, of course, they couldn't say how long but perhaps a week. I went in Freddie's car when he ran my mother back to the nunnery. She begged me to stay with her. "I'll fill a nice hot-water bottle," she said. And when I stood my my ground: "How about my electric blanket?" And I said: "No, Mum, cheero, I'll be in touch", and she started on about lighting the Valor Stove that I loved so much because it threw patterns of light on the bedroom ceiling. I nearly choked with longing for that but I gritted my teeth and said no, the budgie must be fed. And she said she had my old dummy and rattle somewhere—so in the end I ran. Freddie was a hoot. Saying it was a lucky escape and a blessing and stuff like that. I stared through the window at the snowstorm and when we got here, thanked them for all they'd done. Then off they went to the three absolutely gorgeous kiddies—every one a company director—and the oil-fired heating—the labour-saving evergreens—the fibre-glass yacht. I was glad to see the back of him. You can't think with that loud-hailer going on and on. Not that there was *much* to think about. Only details. Our marriage might have worked as well as most if Joe hadn't happened. I was too young for it, that's true of course. I always will be. But Sheila might just have dragged me screaming into manhood. 'Stead of which, I was one of the menagerie. She loved me as much as any goldfish or aphelandra. So now it was a question of how to tell her I was leaving her. And when I went into it, I saw it wouldn't only be about Joe, but also my ambitions—and the first time I saw Father Christmas and—this backache's worse than yesterday and—the pattern on the ceiling—so in the end I better just creep away without a word. (*He goes to the window and opens the curtains. Then he goes into the hall, returns with a case which he puts* L *of the door, picks up one or two objects from the sideboard and tables, and puts them into his pocket*) So I've shaved and washed and packed a case. (*He moves down* C) Haven't decided where I'm going yet. Up the smoke, perhaps, get lost among the Australians. (*He looks at his watch*) Ordinary way I'd be leaving now for eyes-front-hands-on-heads—but never again, I tell you! Want a nice slow job—game-warden—keeper at Regents Park—better still Kew Gardens. (*He turns upstage, looking at the room fixing it for ever*) Well, cheers. (*He turns and smiles to the audience*)

(*There is the sound of the front-door shutting and someone coming into the hall.* BRI *moves up* R *as if to go to the kitchen.* SHEILA *enters up* C *wearing her coat and gloves.* BRI *mimes drawing a gun and firing at her*)

SHEILA. You're up. I thought you'd lie in.
BRI. I've got school.
SHEILA. You're not going?
BRI. Yes.
SHEILA. No. Go absent.
BRI. Only two more days. How are you?
SHEILA. I'm fine—(*moving into the hall*)—thank you. (*She wheels* JOE *in her chair to* C, *turning the chair to face upstage*) There you are, lovely.
BRI. I thought they were keeping her in for a few days.
SHEILA. They wanted to, but what's the point? I've nursed her through pneumonia, 'flu and more colds than I can count. I know the sedation and exercises, why bother busy nurses? Anyway, Dad, did you see the nurses? And the doctors?
BRI. How do you mean, Mum?
SHEILA. Every one a fuzzy-wuzzy.
BRI. I thought it was all right, doctors being black.
SHEILA. She didn't fancy it, Dad. (*She takes off her gloves and starts to unbutton her coat*)
BRI (*to Joe*) How are you, lovely, all right are you?
SHEILA. Still a bit dopey, but her pulse is stronger and she's breathing well. She's as tough as old boots, Dad. She'll get the Queen's telegram yet, you see.

(JOE *moves her head*)

But she's not well enough yet for school. Not this term. And you're not going either. (*She puts her coat on the back of the sofa*)
BRI. I must, Sheila, I must.

Sheila (*moving to Bri and holding him*) Oh Brian, all night I've been thinking that we could spend a few days in bed together. Come on. I'll ring the Head if you're scared.

Bri. Not fair on the other staff.

Sheila. I thought—I'll get home before he's up and make him bacon and eggs and fried apple rings—did you have something hot?

Bri. Tea and toast. I fed the zoo. Tidied up.

Sheila. And I'll take them up to him, and after that I'll climb in with him. What do I find? He's fully dressed. So I have to get all these clothes off him and we'll lie there with the snow outside—and us in there up to our tricks. Last night I lay thinking what you'd tried to do to Joe and I don't blame you, honestly. It was my fault. I've been asking too much.

Bri. Well, I was up the twist—what with Mum, Fred . . .

Sheila. Do you know what I'm going to do? I'm going to look for a residential hospital where she'll be well looked after. When I've found it we're going to leave her there—I don't know—perhaps a month every year. We can go abroad. Haven't been abroad for eleven years. Second honeymoon. Let's start now.

Bri. I'll go and ring the school.

Sheila. All right, but run all the way back—'cos I can't wait long.

(*They break away.* Bri *moves above the sofa to up* c, Sheila *to the kitchen*)

Even though you're not going far I should wrap up warm. It's brilliant sun outside, but treacherous underfoot.

Bri. Yeah, I'll be in the car.

Sheila. What, just to go round there?

Bri. Well, if it's occupied I can try another.

Sheila. Back in one piece, and you be quick. I'll go on up. Carry Joe up when you get back—she's such a lump.

(Sheila *exits to the kitchen.* Bri *looks at Joe, then picks up his case and exits up* c. *The front-door slams.* Sheila *returns*)

Sheila (*picking up her coat, then moving to the fish*) Daddy fed you? He is good. (*To the bird*) Had some seed? What a Daddy! Aren't we lucky!

(Sheila *exits up* c. Joe *remains*)

Curtain

FURNITURE AND PROPERTY LIST

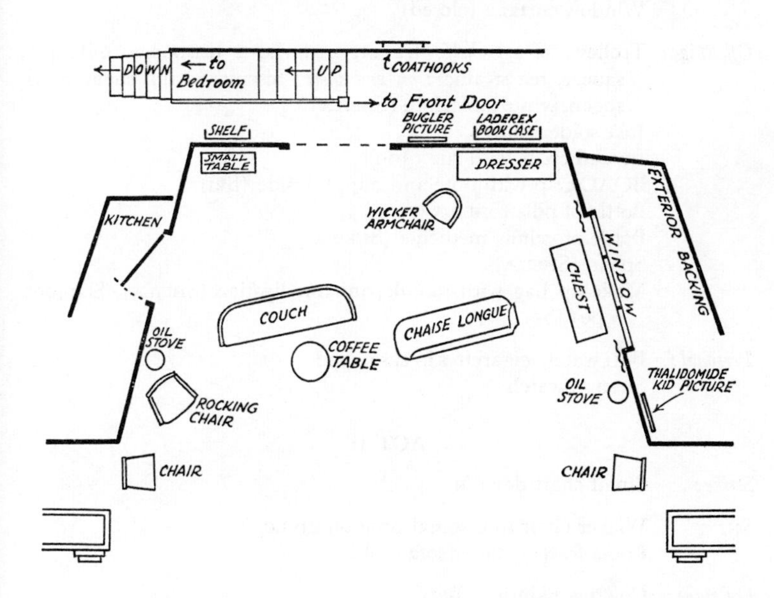

ACT I

On stage: Sofa (RC). *On it:* cushions
Chaise (LC). *On it:* tubular cushion, soft cushion
Rocking chair (R)
Small chair (down R)
Small chair (down L)
Wicker armchair (up LC)
Oil stove (down R)
Oil stove (down L)
Small table (up R). *On it:* small box, magnifying glass, hamster cage, brass table lamp, plants
Coffee table (RC). *On it:* ash-tray, matches
Sideboard (up L). *On it:* goldfish tank, *New Statesman. In cupboard:* bottle of Cyprus sherry, bottle of Spanish cognac, 6 small glasses, blanket
Chest (L). *On it:* television set, *Radio Times,* mouse cage, pot plant
Shelf (up RC). *On it:* bird cage, plants
Bookshelves (on wall up L). *On them:* paperback books, plants, prescription

On walls: cowboy paintings, bugler painting up LC, Thalidomide Kid picture down L
Carpet
Stair carpet
Window curtains (closed)

Off Stage: Trolley: *on 1st shelf:* teapot, 2 mugs, 2 teaspoons, milk jug, saucer, tea strainer: *on 2nd shelf:* biscuits in tin, sugar bowl, spoon, white tablecloth (SHEILA)
Joke spider (BRI)
Invalid chair with rug (JOE)
BOAC grip with note and nappy inside (BRI)
Bottle of pills (SHEILA)
Bottle of yellow medicine (SHEILA)
Spoon (SHEILA)
Make-up bag with nailfile, mirror, lipstick (SHEILA). Skipping rope (JOE)

Personal: BRI: watch, cigarettes in case, pipe
SHEILA: watch

ACT II

Strike: Small chair down R

Set: Wicker chair in original position up LC
Loose feather under sofa cushion

Off stage: Cowboy painting (BRI)
Tray with 4 coffee cups, sugar bowl, 2 spoons, milk jug (SHEILA)
Tartan grip with shopping and cardigan (GRACE)
Empty bottle (SHEILA)
Bottle of yellow medicine (PAM)
Suitcase (BRI)

Personal: PAM: cigarettes in case, watch
FREDDIE: matches, coins
GRACE: handkerchief, handbag with milk check, coins, cosmetic articles, mirror
BRI: old prescription, coins

LIGHTING PLOT

Property fittings required: pendant, brass table lamp

Interior. A sitting-room. The same scene throughout

THE APPARENT SOURCES OF LIGHT are a pendant (C), a table lamp (up R)
THE MAIN ACTING AREAS are RC, up RC, up C, C, extreme down C, LC, down L

ACT I	Night	
To open	Forestage only lit by spot	
Cue 1	BRI exits *Cross-fade to set lighting, pendant and lamp on*	(page 2)
Cue 2	BRI: ". . . talking to the wall" *Bring up downstage lighting*	(page 13)
Cue 3	BRI: "Get back!" *Dim upstage lighting, increase downstage lighting*	(page 14)
Cue 4	SHEILA: ". . . our new G.P." *Take out all upstage lighting*	(page 18)
Cue 5	SHEILA: ". . . being a woman" *Snap on brilliant lighting over whole stage*	(page 29)
Cue 6	JOE exits *Quick fade to Black-out*	(page 29)
ACT II	Night	
To open:	Black-out	
Cue 7	SHEILA turns on hall light *Snap on lighting in hall up* C	(page 30)
Cue 8	SHEILA turns on room lights *Snap on room lighting as Cue* 1	(page 30)
Cue 9	FREDDIE addresses audience *Increase downstage lighting*	(page 33)
Cue 10	FREDDIE: ". . . you're in business" *Reverse Cue* 9	(page 34)
Cue 11	Pam: "Oh, charming" *All upstage lighting out*	(page 44)
Cue 12	PAM: ". . . they were N.P.A." *Bring up general lighting*	(page 44)
Cue 13	GRACE: ". . . Josephine's new cardie" *Repeat Cue* 11	(page 46)
Cue 14	GRACE: ". . . a blooming nun" *Repeat Cue* 12	(page 47)
Cue 15	GRACE exits *All lighting out except spot on rocking chair* R	(page 62)
Cue 16	BRI: ". . . waiting for news" *Spot off rocking chair, spot on downstage area*	(page 62)

Cue 17 BRI: ". . . without a word" (page 63)
Fade to Black-out

Cue 18 BRI opens window curtains (page 63)
Bring up general daytime lighting

Cue 19 SHEILA exits (page 64)
Fade to Black-out as CURTAIN *falls*

EFFECTS PLOT

ACT I

Cue 1 BRI: ". . . hands on heads" (page 1)
School bell rings

Cue 2 SHEILA: ". . . in the first place" (page 6)
Doorbell rings

ACT II

Cue 3 FREDDIE: ". . . . d'you think?" (page 40)
Carol singers start

Cue 4 BRI: ". . . while you were out" (page 41)
Carol singers quieter

Cue 5 FREDDIE: ". . . the special schools" (page 42)
Singers fade

Cue 6 PAM: "God!" (page 42)
Carol singers start "Noel"

Cue 7 SHEILA: "Honestly!" (page 43)
Singers fade

Cue 8 BRI: ". . . doing down here?" (page 45)
Doorbell rings

Cue 9 GRACE: ". . . apart from the sleeves" (page 59)
Explosion and crash

Cue 10 GRACE: ". . . poor Dad had gone" (page 61)
Doorbell rings